Cat Knits

16 Pawsome Knitting Patterns
for Yarn and Cat Lovers

MARNA GILLIGAN

DAVID & CHARLES
www.davidandcharles.com

Contents

Introduction

Welcome to Cat Knits! My completely unscientific survey says that there are many cat-loving knitters and quite a few knitting – and yarn – loving cats. This book should keep everyone happy; lots of quirky, catty knits for the knitters means lots of knitting on the needles, and full knitting needles means plenty of yarn to chase and knitting to nest on for those cats.

Each section of this book uses a different technique spread over four patterns – three accessories and a cardigan or sweater. If you're new to or nervous of that technique you can work your way up to a garment, via accessories, building your skills and confidence, and getting some quick catknitty gratification as you go.

I had a lot of fun dreaming up more ways to put cats on knitting, and my cats had a fine time 'helping' me to knit it all up. I hope you and your feline friends have just as much fun with this book.

Needles and tools

NEEDLE SIZES

Needles have been listed in metric sizes for the projects in this book. If you're used to using US sizes, a conversion chart has been provided here for your reference:

METRIC SIZE	US SIZE
2.75mm	2
3mm	-
3.25mm	3
3.5mm	4
3.75mm	5
4mm	-
4.25mm	6
4.5mm	7
5mm	8
5.5mm	9
6mm	10
6.5mm	10.5
7mm	-
7.5mm	-
8mm	11
9mm	13

The cable lengths used for circular needles are 40cm (16in), 60cm (24in) and 80cm (32in).

STRAIGHT OR CIRCULAR NEEDLES

While a few of the projects in this book can be knit on straight or circular needles, you'll need to use circular needles for anything knit in the round.

The shawls have so many stitches towards the end that they won't fit comfortably on straight needles, although you can, if you prefer, start with straight needles and switch to circular ones later.

SMALL-CIRCUMFERENCE KNITTING

Gloves, hat crowns and sleeves, when knitted in the round, all need small circumference needles. There are a lot of options, and no one right option. I use a mixture of flexible DPNs, regular DPNS (for hat crowns and mitten tips) and tiny circulars (on stranded colourwork these really help me to keep my tension even). Use the method – or methods – you prefer.

Double-pointed needles (DPNs)

These are sets of four or five needles. The stitches are spread across three or four of them, and the remaining needle does the knitting.

Pros: You can look very impressive knitting with so many needles at once! Plus, you have three or four natural break points in your knitting, which can cut down on the need for stitchmarkers, and make projects like hat crowns much easier.

Cons: Knitting on DPNs can be a bit like wrestling with a hedgehog, and you look less impressive when poking yourself with your knitting. Repeatedly. DPNs are also prone to leaving a larger gap at the transitions between needles.

Tip: Ladders between needle changes can be reduced by using five, rather than four, needles, tugging the second stitch on each needle tightly, and by changing the starting point on each needle occasionally.

Magic loop

Magic loop uses a longer length circular needle (often 100cm/40in or more) doubled around itself to create a loop that sits to the side of the work in progress.

Pros: No need to get more needles; the circular needles you've been using for the rest of the project can be used for magic loop. If you're knitting on the go it's very easy to secure your stitches.

Cons: Constantly stopping to rearrange the cable can disrupt your happy knitting rhythm.

Tip: A very flexible cable makes magic loop much, much easier.

Two circular needles

This is similar to magic loop, but using a second needle instead of making a loop.

Pros: Again, no need to buy extra needles – and although you do need two, they don't need to be the same length.

Cons: WIth four needle tips on the loose it can be easy to knit with the wrong one.

Tip: Using needles with different coloured cables can help avoid mixing them up and knitting onto the wrong needle.

Tiny circular needles

These are very short circular needles.

Pros: No faffing about with extra loops of cable or many needles – you can just knit around and around.

Cons: The tiny needles can be difficult to grip.

Tip: Use the longest tiny needle that's still small enough for your project; that extra centimetre or two of grippable needle can be the difference between happy and sad hands.

Flexible DPNs

These are double pointed needle with a flex in them. The stiches are divided between two needles, and you knit around with a third.

Pros: Speedy, but without the hedgehog-wrestling experience of DPNs.

Cons: These are quite expensive, and not very common (yet).

Tip: Like DPNs, gaps in the space between needles can be a problem. Tugging the second stitch, and changing the transition point can help.

Crochet hook

A couple of crochet hooks are an essential part of the knitter's toolkit. They're very useful for catching the occasional dropped stitch, making a provisional cast on, and weaving in ends, as well as reinforcing a steek.

Tapestry needle

For weaving in ends, attaching buttons, and seaming up your knits. The blunt tip helps avoid splitting the yarn you're weaving into.

Stitchmarkers

Stitchmarkers can help keep track of your knitting. Place them onto your needle to identify the beginning of your rounds, mark the place where you'll be working decreases or increases, and to keep track of lace repeats. It can help to have markers of a few different styles – you'll often have both end of round and decrease/ increase points, and using different markers for each of these minimises mix-ups. Pretty stitchmarkers also add a little excitement to your knitting.

Locking markers or bulb pins

These hook onto a stitch, rather than the needle. Pop one onto the stitch you make after every sleeve increase or decrease, and you'll be able to see at a glance the number of increases or decreases you've worked – and quickly count back the rows since your last decrease. They're also excellent for marking short row turns and for securing a dropped stitch until you can pick it up.

Scissors

A small and sharp pair of scissors makes steeking much easier – and, of course, scissors are essential for cutting those ends.

Yarn

Choosing yarn

If you're not sure if a yarn works for your pattern – swatch! And then treat the swatch just as you'll treat the finished project. Pop it in the washing machine if you're planning to machine wash your finished project, soak it and block it if you're planning to handwash. (Let the cat play with it if your cats – like mine – regularly nest in your handknits.)

I treat swatches almost like a map key to the finished knit, and add a little bit of everything the pattern calls for. Try out any new-to-you stitch patterns, add a buttonband and buttonholes, check that your colour choices knit up happily together. And if your pattern uses a steek, then steek your swatch; this lets you check that it will steek safely, and if you're nervous about steeking it will give you a little boost of confidence.

The patterns in this book are all designed to work with standard weight yarns. If you'd like to use a different yarn just make sure that you're using the same weight - and remember that swatching is even more important when you're substituting yarn.

Choosing colours

When picking colours for colourwork you need a bit of contrast between them. There's a quick way to check this; photograph them together, and then reduce the saturation on the photo to grey. Do they still look different? Great! You're all set! Similar colours (two blues, for example) need a little more contrast, while already-contrasting colours can get away with a little less.

It's always worth knitting a little colourwork swatch to check that you're happy with your colour choices.

Abbreviations

k: knit.

k2tog: knit two stitches together as one.

kyok: (k1, yo, k1) into 1 stitch.

m: marker.

m1: make one: with left needle pick up a loop between stitches from the front, then knit into the back of it.

m1o: make one open: with left needle pick up a loop between stitches from the front, then knit into the front of it.

m1p: make one purlwise: with left needle pick up a loop between stitches from the back, then purl into the front of it.

p: purl.

pm: place marker.

p2tog: purl two stitches together as one.

pyop: (p1, yo, p1) into 1 stitch.

RS: right side.

slm: slip marker.

ssk: slip, slip, knit: slip two stitches to right needle as if to knit (one at a time), slip them together back to the left needle, then knit them together through back of loops.

st(s): stitch(es).

tbl: through back of loop.

WS: wrong side.

yo: yarn over.

Skill levels

All of the patterns in this book have been assigned a skill level to help you to identify the ones best suited to your knitting ability. The different levels are indicated by the following icons:

 Perfect patterns for meeting new techniques or for quick-ish knits.

 Build on your experience with these intermediate patterns.

 Looking for a challenge? Try one of the more complex garments.

FAT
CATS

Would you like some cosy feline company? These cats will keep you warm! These patterns use texture to create subtle cat faces and, because they're made with chunky yarn, they're lovely quick knits.

Cosy Cat Sweater

This is a cozy winter sweater, with a yoke of textured cats to keep you warm, and little cats tucked onto the cuffs and hem.

DIMENSIONS

These are the dimensions of the completed sweater. Choose a size with 10-20cm (4-8in) positive ease for a relaxed knit (perfect for winter layering) or knit a size nearer to your own chest size for a snug, fitted sweater.

	SIZE 1	SIZE 2	SIZE 3	SIZE 4	SIZE 5	SIZE 6	SIZE 7	SIZE 8
A: CHEST	90cm (36in)	100cm (40in)	110cm (44in)	120cm (48in)	130cm (52in)	140cm (56in)	150cm (60in)	160cm (64in)
B: NECK TO HEM *(at front)*	60cm (24in)	60.5cm (24¼in)	61cm (24½in)	61cm (24½in)	61.5cm (24½in)	62cm (24¾in)	62.5cm (25in)	63cm (24¼in)
C: YOKE DEPTH	20cm (8in)	21.5cm (8½in)	23cm (9¼in)	24cm (9½in)	25.5cm (10¼in)	27cm (10¾in)	28.5cm (11½in)	30cm (12in)
D: ARM LENGTH *(underarm to cuff)*	48cm (19¼in)	47cm (18¾in)	46cm (18½in)	45cm (18in)	44cm (17½in)	43cm (17¼in)	42cm (16¾in)	41cm (16½in)
E: UPPER ARM *(circumference)*	30cm (12in)	33cm (13¼in)	36cm (14½in)	39cm (15½in)	42cm (16¾in)	45cm (18in)	49cm (19½in)	52cm (20¾in)

GAUGE

14 sts and 18 rows to 10cm (4in) over stocking stitch. Check your gauge in the round, over both large- and small-circumference knitting, and wash and block your swatch before measuring.

GAUGE IS ESSENTIAL TO GET THE RIGHT SIZE.

NEEDLES

- 6mm or size needed to obtain gauge: 40cm, 60-80cm circular needles, and your preferred needles for working a small circumference.
- 5.5mm or one size below that needed to obtain gauge: 40cm, 60-80cm circular needles, and your preferred needles for working a small circumference.

TOOLS AND NOTIONS

- Tapestry needle.
- Three stitchmarkers – one to mark the end of round, and two (cat-markers) to mark the borders of the little inset cats.

YARN

Eden Cottage Yarns Pendle Chunky: 100% superwash merino; 100m (109yds) per 100g; colourway Silver Birch: [8, 8, 9, 9] [10, 11, 11, 12] skeins.

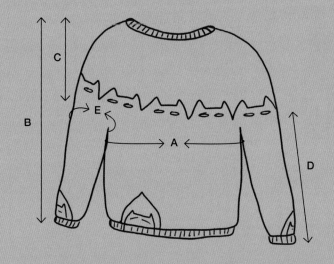

Notes

This sweater is knitted bottom up. The body and the sleeves are worked separately and joined to work the yoke.

Written and charted instructions are both included for the cats; you can work either option.

INSTRUCTIONS

Cast on body

Using below-gauge, longer length circular needle, and the cable cast on method (see Techniques: Cable cast on), cast on [128, 140, 156, 168] [184, 196, 212, 224] stitches.

Join for working in the round (see Techniques: Working in the round), taking care that the stitches are not twisted, and place a marker to indicate the start of the round.

Twisted rib hem

Twisted rib: (K2 tbl, p2) to end of round.

Work a total of six rounds of **Twisted rib**.

Little hem cat

Switch to gauge-sized needle.

Now work either from the **Little hem cat written instructions** or the **Little hem cat chart**.

Little hem cat written instructions

Round 1: K [76, 84, 92, 100] [108, 116, 124, 132], place cat-marker 1 (CM1), k2, p2, k10, p2, k2, place cat-marker 2 (CM2), k to end.

Round 2: K to CM1, slm, k2, p2, k10, p2, k2, slm, k to end.

Rounds 3 to 7: Repeat **Round 2**.

Round 8: K to CM1, slm, (k2, p2) four times, k2, slm, k to end.

Round 9: Repeat **Round 2**.

Round 10: K to CM1, slm, k2, p2, m1p, ssk, k6, k2tog, m1p, p2, k2, slm, k to end.

Round 11: K to CM1, slm, k2, p3, k8, p3, k2, slm, k to end.

Round 12: K to CM1, slm, k2, p3, k1, k2tog, m1p, p2, m1p, ssk, k1, p3, k2, slm, k to end.

Round 13: K to CM1, slm, k1, m1, ssk, p2, m1p, ssk, p4, k2tog, m1p, p2, k2tog, m1, k1, slm, k to end.

Round 14: K to CM1, slm, k2, m1, ssk, p10, k2tog, m1, k2, slm, k to end.

Round 15: K to CM1, slm, k3, m1, ssk, p8, k2tog, m1, k3, slm, k to end.

Round 16: K to CM1, slm, k4, m1, ssk, p6, k2tog, m1, k4, slm, k to end.

Round 17: K to CM1, slm, k5, m1, ssk, p4, k2tog, m1, k5, slm, k to end.

Round 18: K to CM1, slm, k6, m1, ssk, p2, k2tog, m1, k6, slm, k to end.

Round 19: K to CM1, slm, k7, m1, ssk, k2tog, m1, k7, slm, k to end.

Little hem cat chart

Round 1: K [76, 84, 92, 100] [108, 116, 124, 132], place cat-marker 1 (CM1), work row 1 of the little hem cat chart from right to left over the next 18 stitches, place cat-marker 2 (CM2), k to end.

Rounds 2 to 19: K to CM1, slm, work the relevant row of the **Little hem cat chart**, slm, k to end.

Continue body

Remove CM1 and CM2, and work in stocking stitch until the work measures [40, 39, 38, 37] [36, 35, 34, 33]cm ([16, 15½, 15¼, 14¾] [14½, 14, 13½, 13¼]in) from cast on edge, or your desired length.

Set aside.

LITTLE HEM CAT CHART

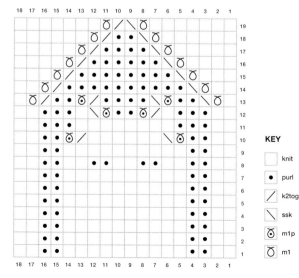

KEY

☐	knit
•	purl
╱	k2tog
╲	ssk
♉	m1p
♉	m1

Cast on sleeves

Using below-gauge needles for working a small-circumference, and the cable cast on method, cast on [28, 28, 32, 32] [36, 36, 40, 40] stitches.

Join for working in the round, taking care that the stitches are not twisted, and place a marker to indicate the start of the round.

Twisted rib cuff

Twisted rib: P1, (k2 tbl, p2) until 3 sts remain, k2 tbl, p1.

Work a total of six rounds of **Twisted rib**.

Little sleeve cat and sleeve shaping

Sleeve shaping for most sizes starts before the little sleeve cat is completed, so check the sleeve shaping for your size now.

Switch to gauge-sized needles.

Now work either from the **Little sleeve cat written instructions** or the **Little sleeve cat chart**.

Little sleeve cat written instructions

Round 1: K [5, 5, 7, 7] [9, 9, 11, 11], place cat-marker 1 (CM1), k2, p2, k10, p2, k2, place cat-marker 2 (CM2), k to end.

Round 2: K to CM1, slm, k1, m1, k1, p2, k10, p2, k1, m1, k1, slm, k to end.

Round 3: K to CM1, slm, k3, p2, k10, p2, k3, slm, k to end.

Round 4: Repeat **Round 3**.

Round 5: K to CM1, slm, k1, m1, k2, p2, k10, p2, k2, m1, k1, slm, k to end.

Round 6: K to CM1, slm, k4, p2, k10, p2, k4, slm, k to end.

Round 7: Repeat **Round 6**.

Round 8: K to CM1, slm, k1, m1, k3, (p2, k2) three times, p2, k3, m1, k1, slm, k to end.

Round 9: K to CM1, slm, k5, p2, k10, p2, k5, slm, k to end.

Round 10: K to CM1, slm, k5, p2, m1p, ssk, k6, k2tog, m1p, p2, k5, slm, k to end.

Round 11: K to CM1, slm, k5, p3, k8, p3, k5, slm, k to end.

Round 12: K to CM1, slm, k5, p3, k1, k2tog, m1p, p2, m1p, ssk, k1, p3, k5, slm, k to end.

Round 13: K to CM1, slm, k4, m1, ssk, p2, m1p, ssk, p4, k2tog, m1p, p2, k2tog, m1, k4, slm, k to end.

Round 14: K to CM1, slm, k5, m1, ssk, p10, k2tog, m1, k5, slm, k to end.

Round 15: K to CM1, slm, k6, m1, ssk, p8, k2tog, m1, k6, slm, k to end.

Round 16: K to CM1, slm, k7, m1, ssk, p6, k2tog, m1, k7, slm, k to end.

Round 17: K to CM1, slm, k8, m1, ssk, p4, k2tog, m1, k8, slm, k to end.

Round 18: K to CM1, slm, k9, m1, ssk, p2, k2tog, m1, k9, slm, k to end.

Round 19: K to CM1, slm, k10, m1, ssk, k2tog, m1, k10, slm, k to end.

Little sleeve cat chart

Round 1: K [5, 5, 7, 7] [9, 9, 11, 11], place cat-marker 1 (CM1), work row 1 of the **Little sleeve cat chart** from right to left over the next 18 stitches, place cat-marker 2 (CM2), k to end.

Rounds 2 to 19: K to CM1, slm, work the relevant row of the **Little sleeve cat chart**, slm, k to end.

Sleeve shaping

On round [24, 18, 18, 14] [13, 11, 11, 11) begin rest of the shaping.

Increase round: K1, m1, k to one before end (working the little sleeve cat where necessary), m1, k1.

Work a total of [3, 5, 5, 7] [9, 11, 11, 13] **Increase rounds**, working [17, 11, 11, 7] [6, 4, 4, 3] rounds between each increase round.

Continue sleeve

Once the little sleeve cat is complete, remove CM1 and CM2 and continue to work the sleeve shaping until complete. *[40, 44, 48, 52] [60, 64, 68, 72] sts*

Continue working straight until sleeve measures [48, 47, 46, 45] [44, 43, 42, 41]cm ([19¼, 18¾, 18½, 18] [17½, 17¼, 16¾, 16½]in) from cast on edge, or your desired length.

Set aside and work a second identical sleeve.

LITTLE SLEEVE CAT CHART

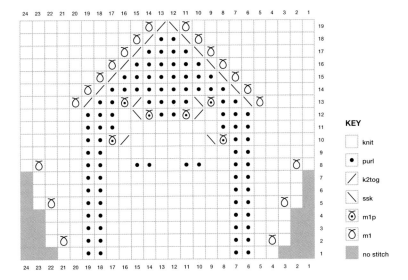

KEY

☐	knit
•	purl
╱	k2tog
╲	ssk
⊘	m1p
♈	m1
▨	no stitch

Join sleeves and body

Using the gauge size, longer length circular needle, and slipping stitches purlwise without knitting them;

- Slip [30, 33, 37, 40] [44, 46, 50, 53] stitches from the sweater body onto the circular needle, and set the next [4, 4, 4, 4] [4, 6, 6, 6] body stitches aside onto scrap yarn.
- Set the first and last [2, 2, 2, 2] [2, 3, 3, 3] stitches of the first sleeve onto scrap yarn, and slip the remaining [36, 40, 44, 48] [56, 58, 62, 66] sleeve stitches onto the circular needle.
- Slip the next [60, 66, 74, 80] [88, 92, 100, 106] stitches from the body onto the circular needle, and set the next [4, 4, 4, 4] [4, 6, 6, 6] body stitches aside onto scrap yarn.
- Set the first and last [2, 2, 2, 2] [2, 3, 3, 3] stitches of the second sleeve onto scrap yarn, and slip the remaining [36, 40, 44, 48] [56, 58, 62, 66] sleeve stitches onto the circular needle.
- Slip the final [30, 33, 37, 40] [44, 46, 50, 53] stitches from the sweater body onto the circular needle.
- Place a marker to indicate the start of round.

[192, 212, 236, 256] [288, 300, 324, 344] sts

Begin yoke

Knit three rounds.

Size 1: Knit one round.

Size 2: K26, k2tog, (k51, k2tog) three times. k to end.

Size 3: K29, m1, (k59, m1) three times, k to end.

Size 4: Knit one round.

Size 5: Knit one round.

Size 6: K38, m1, (k75, m1) three times, k to end.

Size 7: K39, k2tog, (k79, k2tog) three times, k to end.

Size 8: K21, k2tog, (k41, k2tog) seven times, k to end.

[192, 208, 240, 256] [288, 304, 320, 336] sts

It's cat time!

Now work either from the **Yoke cat written instructions** or the **Yoke cat chart**.

Yoke cats written instructions

Round 1: (P1, k14, p1) to end.

Rounds 2 to 5: Repeat **Round 1**.

Round 6: (P1, m1p, ssk, k10, k2tog, m1p, p1) to end.

Round 7: (P2, k12, p2) to end.

Round 8: Repeat **Round 7**.

Round 9: (P2, ssk, k8, k2tog, p2) to end.

[168, 182, 210, 224] [252, 266, 280, 294] sts

Round 10: ((P2, k2) three times, p2) to end.

Round 11: (P2, k10, p2) to end.

Round 12: (P2, m1p, ssk, k6, k2tog, m1p, p2) to end.

Round 13: (P3, k8, p3) to end.

Round 14: (P3, k1, k2tog, m1p, p2, m1p, ssk, k1, p3) to end.

Round 15: (P3, ssk, p4, k2tog, p3) to end.

[144, 156, 180, 192] [216, 228, 240, 252] sts

Yoke cats chart

Working from right to left, repeat each chart row a total of [12, 13, 15, 16] [18, 19, 20, 21] times around the yoke.

[144, 156, 180, 192] [216, 228, 240, 252] sts

Yoke decreases

Purl [3, 3, 4, 5] [5, 5, 6, 6] rounds.

Decrease round one

P2, (p2tog, p4) until 4 sts remain, p2tog, p2. *[120, 130, 150, 160] [180, 190, 200, 210] sts*

Purl [3, 3, 4, 4] [5, 5, 6, 6] rounds.

Decrease round two

P2, (p2tog, p3) until 3 sts remain, p2tog, p1. *[96, 104, 120, 128] [144, 152, 160, 168] sts*

Purl [3, 3, 4, 4] [5, 5, 5, 6] rounds.

YOKE CATS CHART

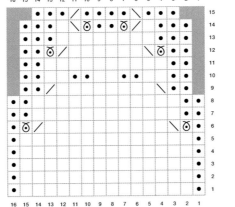

KEY

☐	knit
•	purl
╱	k2tog
╲	ssk
⊘	m1p
▨	no stitch

Decrease round three

(P2, p2tog) to end of round. *[72, 78, 90, 96] [108, 114, 120, 126] sts*

Purl one round.

Short row shaping

Purl [24, 26, 30, 32] [36, 38, 40, 42] sts, wrap and turn (see Techniques: Short rows).

Knit [48, 52, 60, 64] [72, 76, 80, 84] sts, wrap and turn.

Purl back to end of round maker.

Purl one round, picking up and knitting the wrapped stitches as you work.

Purl a further [0, 0. 0, 1] [1, 2, 2, 3] rounds.

Decrease round four

Size 1: Skip forward to **Twisted rib neckband** without working any further rounds.

Size 2: (P2tog, p11) to end.

Size 3: ((P5, p2tog) three times), ((p4, p2tog) four times) twice.

Size 4: (P3, p2tog, p3, p2tog, p3, p2tog, p3, p2tog, p2, p2tog) to end.

Size 5: ((P2, p2tog) six times, p1, p2tog) four times.

Size 6: P6, (p1, p2tog) 17 times, p6, (p1, p2tog) 17 times.

Size 7: (P2, p2tog, p1, p2tog, p1, p2tog) to end.

Size 8: (P1, p2tog) to end.

All sizes: Purl [-, 1, 1, 1] [2, 3, 4, 4] rounds. *[-, 72, 76, 76] [80, 80, 84, 84] sts*

Twisted rib neckband

Switch to below-gauge, 40cm circular needle.

Twisted rib: (K2 tbl, p2) to end.

Work a total of six rounds of **Twisted rib**.

Bind off in pattern (see Techniques: Basic bind off in pattern).

Finishing

Pick up and graft the stitches that were left on hold at each underarm (see Techniques: Grafting).

Weave in ends.

Because the chunky-weight yarn is very heavy when wet this sweater needs to be blocked flat (see Techniques: Blocking). After squeezing any excess water from your sweater, lay it on a towel or blocking mat and shape it to the dimensions in the size chart.

Squishy Cat Shawl

This garter stitch shawl has a border of cat faces around the edge. An i-cord edging finishes it off. It's a cosy shawl, perfect for wrapping yourself up in cold weather.

DIMENSIONS

- Width: 170cm (68in).
- Depth: 45cm (18ln).

GAUGE

10 sts and 14 rows to 10cm (4in) over stocking stitch worked flat.

GAUGE ISN'T ESSENTIAL FOR THIS PROJECT, ALTHOUGH VARIATIONS WILL MEAN A LARGER OR SMALLER SHAWL, AND A LOOSER GAUGE MAY REQUIRE MORE YARN.

NEEDLES

- 7.5mm or size needed to obtain gauge: 80cm or longer circular needle.
- 9mm or two sizes larger than that needed for gauge: any length of circular or straight needles.

TOOLS AND NOTIONS

- Tapestry needle.
- Two stitchmarkers.

YARN

Eden Cottage Yarns Pendle Chunky: 100% superwash merino; 100m (109yds) per 100g; colourway Silver Birch: 6 skeins.

Notes

Written and charted instructions are both included; you can work either option.

INSTRUCTIONS

Cast on and set up

Using gauge size circular needle, and the cable cast on method (see Techniques: Cable cast on), cast on 6 stitches.

Row 1: K2, kyok, kyok, k2. *10 sts*

Row 2: P to end.

Row 3: K1, m1, k1, kyok, k4, kyok, k1, m1, k1. *16 sts*

Row 4: P3, k10, p3.

Row 5: K2, m1, k1, kyok, k8, kyok, k1, m1, k2. *22 sts*

Row 6: P4, k14, p4.

Row 7: K3, m1, k1, kyok, k12, kyok, k1, m1, k3. *28 sts*

Row 8: P5, pm, k18, pm, p5.

Body

Row 1 (RS): K5, slm, kyok, k to 1 st before marker, kyok, slm, k5.

Row 2 (WS): P5, slm, k to m, slm, p5.

Work **Rows 1 and 2** a total of 32 times, ending with a WS row. *156 sts*

Feline preparation

Row 1: K5, slm, kyok, (k11, m1) 12 times, k to 1 st before marker, kyok, slm, k5. *172 sts*

Row 2: P5, slm, k to m, slm. p5.

Row 3: K5, slm, pyop, p to 1 st before marker, pyop, slm, k5. *176 sts*

Row 4: P5, slm, k to m, slm. p5.

Row 5: K5, slm, pyop, p to 1 st before marker, pyop, slm, k5. *180 sts*

Cat time!

Now work either from the **Written instructions** or the **Chart**.

Written instructions

Row 1 (WS): P5, slm, k1, (k6, p1, k10, p1, k6) seven times, k1, slm, p5.

Row 2 (RS): K5, slm, m1, p1, (p6, kyok, p10, kyok, p6) seven times, p1, m1, slm, k5. *210 sts*

Row 3 (WS): P5, slm, p1, k1, (k4, ssk, p3, k2tog, k6, ssk, p3, k2tog, k4) seven times, k1, p1, slm, p5. *182 sts*

Row 4 (RS): K5, slm, m1, k1, p1, (p5, k3, p8, k3, p5) seven times, p1, k1, m1, slm, k5. *184 sts*

Row 5 (WS): P5, slm, p2, k1, (k5, p3, k8, p3, k5) seven times, k1, p2, slm, p5).

Row 6 (RS): K5, slm, m1, k2, p1, (p4, k2tog, m1, k1, m1, ssk, k6, k2tog, m1, k1, m1, ssk, p4) seven times, p1, k2, m1, slm, k5. *186 sts*

Row 7 (WS): P5, slm, p3, k1, (k4, p16, k4) seven times, k1, p3, slm, p5.

Row 8 (RS): K5, slm, m1, k3, p1, (p4, k16, p4) seven times, p1, k3, m1, slm, k5. *188 sts*

Row 9 (WS): P5, slm, k2, p2, k1, (k3, p2tog tbl, m1p, p14, m1p, p2tog, k3) seven times, k1, p2, k2, slm, p5.

Row 10 (RS): K5, slm, m1, k4, p1, (p3, k18, p3) seven times, p1, k4, m1, slm, k5. *190 sts*

Row 11 (WS): P5, slm, p1, k2, p2, k1, (k3, p3, k3, p6, k3, p3, k3) seven times, k1, p2, k2, p1, slm, p5.

Row 12 (RS): K5, slm, m1, k5, p1, (p1, m1p, p1, k2tog, m1, k1, p5, k4, p5, k1, m1, ssk, p1, m1p, p1) seven times, p1, k5, m1, slm, k5. *206 sts*

Row 13 (WS): P5, slm, p2, k2, p2, k1, (k3, p20, k3) seven times, k1, p2, k2, p2, slm, p5.

Row 14 (RS): K5, slm, m1, k6, p1, (p3, k20, p3) seven times, p1, k6, m1, slm, k5. *208 sts*

Row 15 (WS): P5, slm, p3, k2, p2, k1, (k2, p2tog tbl, m1p, p18, m1p, p2tog), k2) seven times, k1, p2, k2, p3, slm, p5.

Row 16 (RS): K5, slm, m1, k7, p1, (p2, k22, p2) seven times, p1, k7, m1, slm, k5. *210 sts*

Row 17 (WS): P5, slm, (K2, p2) twice, k1, (k2, p22, k2) seven times, k1, (p2, k2) twice, slm, p5.

Row 18 (RS): K5, slm, m1, knit to m, m1, slm, k5. *212 sts*

Row 19 (WS): P5, slm, p1, (k2, p2) twice, k1, ((k2, p2) six times, k2) seven times, k1, (p2, k2) twice, p1, slm, p5.

Row 20 (RS): Repeat **Row 18**. *214 sts*

Row 21 (WS): P5, slm, p2, (k2, p2) twice, k1, ((k2, p2,) six times, k2) seven times, k1, (p2, k2) twice, p2, slm, p5.

Row 22 (RS): Repeat **Row 18**. *216 sts*

Row 23 (WS): P5, slm, p3, (k2, p2) twice, k1, ((k2, p2) six times, k2) seven times, k1, (p2, k2) twice, p3, slm, p5.

Row 24 (RS): Repeat **Row 18**. *218 sts*

CAT TIME! CHART

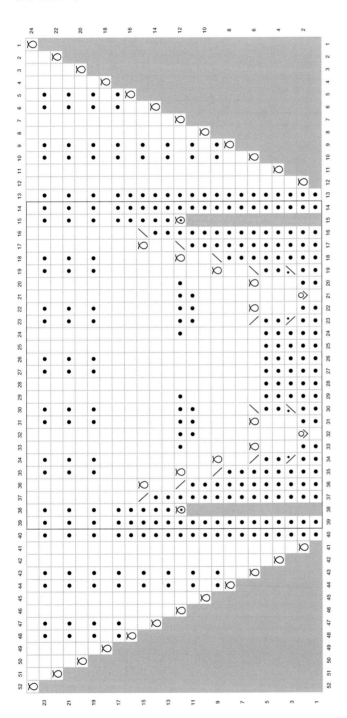

Chart

Work WS (odd numbered) rows from left to right as follows: P5, slm, work from chart, slm, p5.

Work RS (even numbered) rows from right to left as follows: K5, slm, work from chart, slm, k5.

Start with row 1 and repeat the boxed section seven times across the row.

YOU'RE BEGINNING WITH A WRONG SIDE ROW.

Bind off and finishing

Bind off using larger needles and a three-stitch i-cord bindoff (see Techniques: i-cord bindoff).

Weave in ends and block (see Techniques: Blocking) as follows:

After soaking, pin the shawl in a straight line across the top edge, leaving the stocking stitch border to roll naturally. Shape the bottom of the shawl into a wide semi-circle and leave to dry flat.

KEY

	RS: knit WS: purl
•	RS: purl WS: knit
⌽	RS: kyok
\	RS: ssk WS: p2tog tbl
/	RS: k2tog WS: p2tog
⁄	WS: k2tog
\	WS: ssk
○	RS: m1 WS: m1p
⊙	RS: m1p
	no stitch
	repeat

Cuddly Cat Hat

A row of little cats peek out from the brim of this cute hat topped with a cheery pompom.

DIMENSIONS

- Size: [Small, Medium].
- To fit head circumference: [46-53, 54-60] cm ([18½-21¼, 21½-24]in).
- Hat depth (crown to brim): [20, 22]cm ([8, 8¾]in), with a turned brim.

THIS HAT IS DESIGNED TO BE WORN WITH AT LEAST 2.5CM (1IN) STRETCH AT BRIM.

GAUGE

14 sts and 18 rows to 10cm (4in) over stocking stitch worked in the round.

GAUGE IS ESSENTIAL FOR A WELL-FITTING HAT.

NEEDLES

- 6mm or size needed to obtain gauge: 40cm circular needle and your preferred needles for working a small circumference.
- 5.5mm or one size below that needed to obtain gauge: 40cm circular needle.

TOOLS AND NOTIONS

- Tapestry needle.
- One stitchmarker.

YARN

Eden Cottage Yarns Pendle Chunky: 100% superwash merino; 100m (109yds) per 100g; colourway Silver Birch: 1 skein for the hat, plus half a skein for the pompom.

Notes

Written and charted instructions are both included; you can work either option.

INSTRUCTIONS

Cast on and brim

Using the smaller circular needle, and the cable cast on method (see Techniques: Cable cast on), cast on [60, 72] stitches.

Join for working in the round (see Techniques: Working in the round), taking care to not twist the stitches, and place a stitchmarker to mark the start of round.

Twisted rib: P1 tbl, (k2, p2 tbl) until 3 sts remain, k2, p1 tbl.

Work a total of ten rounds of **Twisted rib**.

Knit one round.

Plain rib: P1, (k2, p2) until 3 sts remain, k2, p1.

Work a total of six rounds of **Plain rib**.

Cats!

Switch to the larger circular needle.

Now work either from the **Written instructions** or the **Chart**.

Written instructions

Rounds 1 to 11: (P1, k10, p1) to end.

Round 12: (P1, (k2, p2) twice, k2, p1) to end.

Round 13: Repeat **Round 1**.

Round 14: (P1, m1p, ssk, k6, k2tog, m1p, p1) to end.

Round 15: (P2, k8, p2) to end.

Round 16: (P2, k1, k2tog, m1p, p2, m1p, ssk, k1, p2) to end.

Round 17: (P2, ssk, p4, k2tog, p2) to end. *[50, 60] sts*

Chart

Working from right to left, repeat each chart row [five, six] times around the hat.

Crown decreases

Purl [2, 5] rounds.

Switch to needles for working a small circumference.

Round 1: (P8, p2tog) to end. *[45, 54] sts*

Round 2: Purl one round.

Round 3: (P7, p2tog) to end. *[40, 48] sts*

Round 4: Purl one round.

Round 5: (P6, p2tog) to end. *[35, 42] sts*

Round 6: Purl one round.

Round 7: (P5, p2tog) to end. *[30, 36] sts*

Round 8: (P2tog, p4) to end. *[25, 30] sts*

Round 9: (P3, p2tog) to end. *[20, 24] sts*

Round 10: (P2tog, p2) to end. *[15, 18] sts*

Round 11: (P1, P2tog) to end. *[10, 12] sts*

Round 12: P2tog to end. *[5, 6] sts*

Break yarn and draw through remaining [5, 6] sts, tighten to close.

Finishing

Weave in ends.

Fold the brim over with the crease at the knitted row – it should fold naturally at that point – and block (see Techniques: Blocking).

Make a pompom (see Techniques: Pompoms) and attach it to the crown of the hat.

CATS! CHART

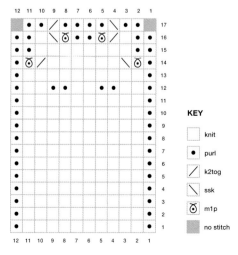

Chunky Cat Cowl

Snow leopards wrap their huge, fluffy tails around their necks to keep warm when it's chilly. This cowl isn't quite as amazing as a snow leopard's tail – what is? – but it will keep your neck cosy in cold weather.

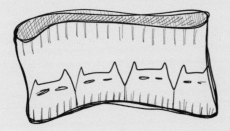

DIMENSIONS

- Circumference: 96cm (38½in).
- Depth: 33cm (13¼in).

GAUGE

10 sts and 14 rows to 10cm (4in) over stocking stitch worked in the round.

GAUGE ISN'T ESSENTIAL FOR THIS PROJECT, ALTHOUGH VARIATIONS WILL MEAN A LARGER OR SMALLER COWL, AND A LOOSER GAUGE MAY REQUIRE MORE YARN.

NEEDLES

- 7.5mm or size needed to obtain gauge: 40cm or 60cm circular needle.

TOOLS AND NOTIONS

- Tapestry needle.
- One stitchmarker.

YARN

Eden Cottage Yarns Pendle Chunky: 100% superwash merino; 100m (109yds) per 100g; colourway Silver Birch: 2 skeins.

Notes

Written and charted instructions are both included; you can work either option.

INSTRUCTIONS

Cast on

Using gauge size circular needle, and the cable cast on method (see Techniques: Cable cast on), cast on 96 stitches.

Join for working in the round (see Techniques: Working in the round), being careful to not twist the stitches, and place a stitchmarker to indicate the start of round.

*Now work either from the **Written instructions** or the **Chart**.*

Written instructions

Shadow rib edging

Round 1: Knit.

Round 2: (P2, k2) to end.

Work **Rounds 1 and 2** a total of five times.

Transition

(P2, k2) to end for two rounds.

Purl for five rounds.

Here come the cats!

Round 1: (P7, kyok, p10, kyok, p5) four times. *112 sts*

Round 2: (P5, p2tog tbl, k3, p2tog, p6, p2tog tbl, k3, p2tog, p3) four times. *96 sts*

Rounds 3 to 4: (P6, k3, p8, k3, p4) four times.

Round 5: (P5, k2tog, m1, k1, m1, ssk, k6, k2tog, m1, k1, m1, ssk, p3) four times.

Rounds 6 to 7: (P5, k16, p3) four times.

Round 8: (P4, k2tog, m1, k14, m1, ssk, p2) four times.

Round 9: (P4, k18, p2) four times.

Round 10: (P4, k3, p3, k6, p3, k3, p2) four times.

Round 11: (P3, k2tog, m1, k1, p5, k4, p5, k1, m1, ssk, p1) four times.

Rounds 12 to 13: (P3, k20, p1) four times.

Round 14: (P2, k2tog, m1, k18, m1, ssk) four times.

Transition

(P2, k22) for five rounds.

Shadow rib edging

Round 1: (P2, k2) to end.

Round 2: Knit.

Work **Rounds 1 and 2** a total of five times.

Chart

Working from right to left, repeat each chart row four times around the cowl.

Repeat the boxed rows the stated number of times in total.

Bind off and finishing

Bind off (see Techniques: Basic bind off).

Weave in ends, and block (see Techniques: Blocking).

COSY CATS CHART

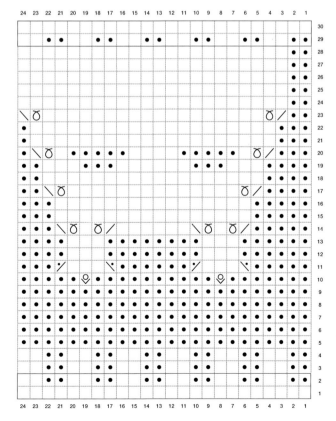

KEY

·	knit
•	purl
⚲	kyok
\	RS: ssk
/	k2tog
·/	p2tog
·\	p2tog tbl
♉	m1
☐	shadow rib: work 5 repeats for a total of 10 rounds

DAINTY
CATS

Small, subtle cats, with a
smattering of pawprints: the
perfect knits for cool summer
evenings. These projects
combine a smidge of colourwork
with some straightforward lace.

Pretty Pawsome Cat Cowl

This is a light and airy lace cowl, with lacy pawprints and tiny peeking cats.

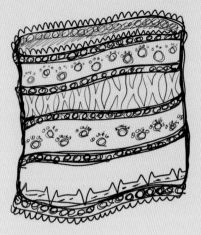

DIMENSIONS

- Circumference: 72cm (28¾in).
- Depth: 39cm (15½in).

GAUGE

20 sts and 26 rows to 10cm (4in) over stocking stitch worked in the round. Wash and gently block your swatch before measuring.

GAUGE ISN'T ESSENTIAL FOR THIS PROJECT, ALTHOUGH VARIATIONS WILL MEAN A LARGER OR SMALLER COWL, AND A LOOSER GAUGE MAY REQUIRE MORE YARN.

NEEDLES

- 3.75mm or size needed to obtain gauge: 40 or 60cm circular needle.

TOOLS AND NOTIONS

- Stitchmarker.
- Tapestry needle.

YARN

Eden Cottage Yarns Milburn 4ply: 85% British Bluefaced Leicester, 15% silk; 200m (218yds) per 50g.

- MC: Thyme: 1 ball.
- CC1: Natural: 1 ball.
- CC2: Tea Rose: 1 ball.
- CC3: Catmint: 1 ball.

Notes

Written and charted instructions are included for the lace sections; you can work from either option.

INSTRUCTIONS

Cast on

Using CC1, and the picot cast on method, cast on 144 stitches (see Techniques: Picot cast on).

Join for working in the round, being careful to not twist the stitches, and place a marker to mark the start of round (see Techniques: Working in the round).

Eyelets

Eyelet round 1: Knit to end.

Eyelet round 2: Purl to end.

Eyelet round 3: (K2tog, yo) to end.

Eyelet round 4: Purl to end.

Toebeans part one

Switch to MC.

Now work either from the **Toebeans written instructions** or from the **Toebeans chart**.

There's a double yarnover in this section – be careful to knit into the front of the first half, and the back of the second half of this on the following round.

Toebeans written instructions

Rounds 1 and 2: Knit.

Round 3: (K1, yo, ssk, k2tog, yo, k7) twelve times.

Round 4: Knit.

Round 5: (Yo, ssk, k2, k2tog, yo, k6) twelve times.

Round 6: Knit.

Round 7: (K1, k2tog, yo, yo, ssk, k7) twelve times.

Round 8: (K2, knit into the front and back of the double yarnover, k8) twelve times.

Round 9: Knit.

Round 10: (K7, yo, ssk, k2tog, yo, k1) twelve times.

Round 11: Knit.

Round 12: (K6, yo, ssk, k2, k2tog, yo) twelve times.

Round 13: Knit.

Round 14: (K7, k2tog, yo, yo, ssk, k1) twelve times.

Round 15: (K8, knit into the front and back of the double yarnover, k2) twelve times.

Round 16: Knit.

Toebeans chart

Starting from the bottom and working from right to left, repeat each **Toebeans chart** row 12 times around the cowl.

TOEBEANS CHART

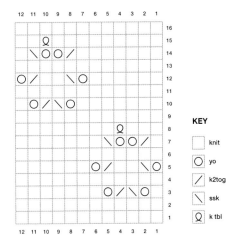

					KEY
		knit
O		yo
/		k2tog
\		ssk
Ω		k tbl

Eyelets

Switch to CC1, and repeat **Eyelet rounds 1 to 4**.

Waving tails

Switch to CC2.

Now work either from the **Waving tails written instructions** or from the **Waving tails chart**.

Waving tails written instructions

Round 1: (P1, k2, p7, k2) twelve times.

Rounds 2 and 3: Repeat **Round 1**.

Round 4: (P1, yo, k1, ssk, p5, k2tog, k1, yo) twelve times.

Round 5: (P2, k2, p5, k2, p1) twelve times.

Round 6: (P2, yo, k1, ssk, p3, k2tog, k1, yo, p1) twelve times.

Round 7: ((P3, k2) twice, p2) twelve times.

Round 8: (P3, yo, k1, ssk, p1, k2tog, k1, yo, p2) twelve times.

Rounds 9 to 11: (P4, k2, p1, k2, p3) twelve times.

Round 12: (P3, k2tog, k1, yo, p1, yo, k1, ssk, p2) twelve times.

Round 13: Repeat **Round 7**.

Round 14: (P2, k2tog, k1, yo, p3, yo, k1, ssk, p1) twelve times.

Round 15: Repeat **Round 5**.

Round 16: (P1, k2tog, k1, yo, p5, yo, k1, ssk) twelve times.

Rounds 17 to 19: Repeat **Round 1**.

Waving tails chart

Starting from the bottom and working from right to left, repeat each **Waving tails chart** row 12 times around the cowl.

Eyelets

Switch to CC1, and repeat **Eyelet rounds 1 to 4**.

Toebeans part two

Switch to MC and work the **Toebeans written instructions** or the **Toebeans chart** again.

Eyelets

Switch to CC1, and repeat **Eyelet rounds 1 to 4**.

Tiny cats are watching

Continuing in CC1, knit for six rounds.

Work the **Little cat chart**, starting from the bottom right, and working a total of eighteen repeats, bringing in CC3 where indicated (see Techniques: Stranded colourwork).

MAKE SURE THAT YOUR COLOURWORK TENSION IS VERY LOOSE HERE.

WAVING TAILS CHART

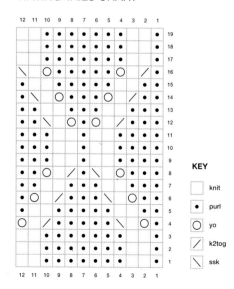

LITTLE CAT CHART

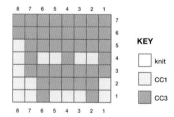

Eyelets

Continuing with CC1, work a final repeat of **Eyelet rounds 1 to 4**.

Knit one round.

Bind off using a picot bind off (see Techniques: Picot bind off).

Finishing

Weave in all ends, and block to the dimensions in the diagram; the lacework will benefit from being stretched a bit (see Techniques: Blocking).

Tiny Cats Cardigan

A light, fitted cardigan, with a pawprint lace yoke and a smattering of little cats.

DIMENSIONS

	SIZE 1	SIZE 2	SIZE 3	SIZE 4	SIZE 5	SIZE 6	SIZE 7	SIZE 8
A: CHEST	75cm (30in)	80cm (32in)	85cm (34in)	90cm (36in)	95cm (38in)	100cm (40in)	105cm (42in)	110cm (44in)
B: YOKE DEPTH	19cm (7½in)	19.5cm (7¾in)	20cm (8in)	21cm (8½in)	21.5cm (8½in)	22cm (8¾in)	23cm (9¼in)	23.5cm (9½in)
C: SLEEVE TOP	29cm (11½in)	30.5cm (12¼in)	32cm (12¾in)	33.5cm (13½in)	34cm (13½in)	35.5cm (14¼in)	37cm (14¾in)	38.5cm (15½in)
D: SLEEVE LENGTH	44cm (17½in)	43.5cm (17½in)	42.5cm (17in)	42cm (16¾in)	41cm (16½in)	40.5cm (16¼in)	39.5cm (15¾in)	39cm (15½in)
E: BODY LENGTH	35cm (14in)	35cm (14in)	34.5cm (13¾in)	34.5cm (13¾in)	34cm (13½in)	33.5cm (13½in)	33cm (13¼in)	32.5cm (13in)

	SIZE 9	SIZE 10	SIZE 11	SIZE 12	SIZE 13	SIZE 14	SIZE 15	SIZE 16
A: CHEST	115cm (46in)	120cm (48in)	125cm (50in)	130cm (52in)	135cm (54in)	140cm (56in)	145cm (58in)	150cm (60in)
B: YOKE DEPTH	24cm (9½in)	25cm (10in)	25.5cm (10¼in)	26cm (10½in)	27cm (10¾in)	27.5cm (11in)	28cm (11¼in)	29cm (11½in)
C: SLEEVE TOP	40cm (16in)	41.5cm (16½in)	43cm (17¼in)	44.5cm (17¾in)	46cm (18½in)	47.5cm (19in)	49cm (19½in)	50.5cm (20¼in)
D: SLEEVE LENGTH	38.5cm (15½in)	38cm (15¼in)	37.5cm (15in)	37cm (14¾in)	36.5cm (14½in)	36cm (14½in)	35.5cm (14¼in)	34.5cm (13¾in)
E: BODY LENGTH	32.5cm (13in)	32cm (12¾in)	31.5cm (12½in)	31.5cm (12½in)	30.5cm (12¼in)	30.5cm (12¼in)	30cm (12in)	29.5cm (11¾in)

GAUGE

26 sts and 32 rows to 10cm (4in) over stocking stitch worked in the round. Check your gauge in the round, over both large- and small-circumference knitting, and wash and block your swatch before measuring.

GAUGE IS ESSENTIAL TO GET THE RIGHT SIZE.

NEEDLES

- 3mm or size needed to obtain gauge: 40cm and 80cm circular needles, and your preferred needles for working a small circumference.

- 2.75mm or one size below that needed for gauge: 40cm and 80cm circular needles, and your preferred needles for working a small circumference.

- 3.25mm or one size above that needed for gauge: 40cm or longer circular needle – for casting on the neck, and binding off the hem and cuffs.

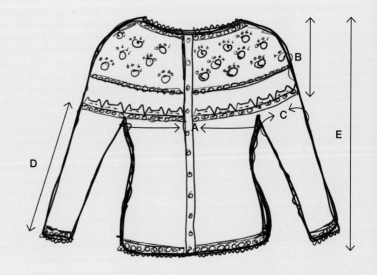

TOOLS AND NOTIONS

- Stitchmarkers.
- Locking markers or bulb pins – for keeping track of increases and decreases, and marking buttonhole positions.
- Scrap yarn – for holding stitches.
- A crochet hook: a size or two smaller than your gauge needle size – for reinforcing the steek.
- Small, sharp scissors for steeking.
- Tapestry needle.
- 12-16 Buttons to fit your buttonholes – about 15mm (⅝in).

YARN

Eden Cottage Yarns Milburn 4ply: 85% British Bluefaced Leicester, 15% silk; 200m (218yds) per 50g.

- MC: Thyme: [5, 5, 5, 5] [5, 6, 6, 6] [6, 6, 6, 6] [6, 7, 7, 7] balls.
- CC1: Natural: [2, 2, 2, 2] [2, 2, 2, 2] [2, 2, 3, 3] [3, 3, 3, 3] balls.
- CC2: Tea Rose: [1, 1, 1, 2] [2, 2, 2, 2] [2, 2, 2, 3] [3, 3, 3, 3] balls.
- CC3: Catmint: 1 ball.

Notes

Construction

The first part of the yoke expands with frequent increase rounds – when you get to the stopping point for your size you'll be directed to skip forward to the short rows. The yoke also increases as you knit the cats, but at a slightly slower pace.

Steek stitches

The steek stitches aren't counted in the main stitch counts. They should be knit in every round, and worked in pattern over the colourwork sections.

INSTRUCTIONS

Cast on and neckband

Using CC1, the above-gauge needles, and a loose cast on method, cast on [130, 130, 130, 130] [130, 138, 138, 138] [138, 138, 138, 146] [146, 146, 146, 146] stitches (see Techniques: Loose cast on).

Switch to the below-gauge needles, and work four rows of stocking stitch, beginning with a RS row.

Picot edge

Switch to the gauge-sized needles.

Picot Edge: K1, (yo, k2tog) until 1 st remains, yo, k1.

[131, 131, 131, 131] [131, 139, 139, 139] [139, 139, 139, 147] [147, 147, 147, 147] sts

Switch to CC2, and break CC1.

Purl one row.

Knit one row.

Place marker, cast on five steek stitches (see Techniques: Standard cast on), place marker, and join for working in the round (see Techniques: Working in the round).

Work six rounds in stocking stitch.

Eyelets

Switch to CC1.

Round 1: Purl.

Round 2: K1, (yo, k2tog) until 2 sts remain, yo, k2.

Round 3: Purl.

Round 4: Knit.

[132, 132, 132, 132] [132, 140, 140, 140] [140, 140, 140, 148] [148, 148, 148, 148] sts (and 5 steek sts)

Yoke increases

There's a double yarnover in this section – be careful to knit into the front of the first half, and the back of the second half of this on the following round.

Increase section one

Switch to CC2.

Knit three rounds.

Next round: K2, (k3, m1, k2, m1, k3) until 2 sts remain, k2.

Knit one round.

[164, 164, 164, 164] [164, 174, 174, 174] [174, 174, 174, 184] [184, 184, 184, 184] sts (and 5 steek sts)

Increase section two

Round 1: K2, (k3, yo, ssk, k2tog, yo, k3) until 2 sts remain, k2.

Round 2: Knit.

Round 3: K2, (k2, yo, ssk, k2, k2tog, yo, k2) until 2 sts remain, k2.

Round 4: Knit.

Round 5: K2, (k5, yo, yo, k5) until 2 sts remain, k2.

Round 6: K2, (k5, knit into the front and back of the double yarnover, k5) until 2 sts remain, k2.

[196, 196, 196, 196] [196, 208, 208, 208] [208, 208, 208, 220] [220, 220, 220, 220] sts (and 5 steek sts)

Increase section three

Round 1: K8, (k4, yo, ssk, k2tog, yo, k4) until 8 sts remain, k8.

Round 2: Knit.

Round 3: K8, (k3, yo, ssk, k2, k2tog, yo, k3) until 8 sts remain, k8.

Round 4: Knit.

Round 5: K8, (k6, yo, yo, k6) until 8 sts remain, k8.

Round 6: K8, (K6, knit into the front and back of the double yarnover, k6) until 8 sts remain, k8.

[226, 226, 226, 226] [226, 240, 240, 240] [240, 240, 240, 254] [254, 254, 254, 254] sts (and 5 steek sts)

Increase section four

Round 1: K1, (k5, yo, ssk, k2tog, yo, k5) until 1 st remains, k1.

Round 2: Knit.

Round 3: K1, (k4, yo, ssk, k2, k2tog, yo, k4) until 1 st remains, k1.

Round 4: Knit.

Round 5: K1, (k7, yo, yo, k7) until 1 st remains, k1.

Round 6: K1, (k7, knit into the front and back of the double yarnover, k7) until 1 st remains, k1.

[258, 258, 258, 258] [258, 274, 274, 274] [274, 274, 274, 290] [290, 290, 290, 290] sts (and 5 steek sts)

Size 1: skip forward to Tiny cats setup.

Increase section five
(sizes 2+ only)

Round 1: K9, (k6, yo, ssk, k2tog, yo, k6) until 9 sts remain, k9.

Round 2: Knit.

Round 3: K9, (k5, yo, ssk, k2, k2tog, yo, k5) until 9 sts remain, k9.

Round 4: Knit.

Round 5: K9, (k8, yo, yo, k8) until 9 sts remain, k9.

Round 6: K9, (k8, knit into the front and back of the double yarnover, k8) until 9 sts remain, k9.

[-, 288, 288, 288] [288, 306, 306, 306] [306, 306, 306, 324] [324, 324, 324, 324] sts (and 5 steek sts)

Sizes 2 and 3: skip forward to Tiny cats setup.

Increase section six
(sizes 4+ only)

Round 1: (k7, yo, ssk, k2tog, yo, k7) to end.

Round 2: Knit.

Round 3: (k6, yo, ssk, k2, k2tog, yo, k6) to end.

Round 4: Knit.

Round 5: (k9, yo, yo, k9) to end.

Round 6: (k9, knit into the front and back of the double yarnover, k9) to end.

[-, -, -, 320] [320, 340, 340, 340] [340, 340, 340, 360] [360, 360, 360, 360] sts (and 5 steek sts)

Sizes 4 to 7: skip forward to Tiny cats setup.

Increase section seven
(sizes 8+ only)

Round 1: K10, (k8, yo, ssk, k2tog, yo, k8) until 10 sts remain, k10.

Round 2: Knit.

Round 3: K10, (k7, yo, ssk, k2, k2tog, yo, k7) until 10 sts remain, k10.

Round 4: Knit.

Round 5: K10, (k10, yo, yo, k10) until 10 sts remain, k10.

Round 6: K10, (k10, knit into the front and back of the double yarnover, k10) until 10 sts remain, k10.

[-, -, -, -] [-, -, -, 372] [372, 372, 372, 394] [394, 394, 394, 394] sts (and 5 steek sts)

Sizes 8 and 9: skip forward to Tiny cats setup.

Increase section eight
(sizes 10+ only)

Round 1: K8, yo, ssk, k2tog, yo, k9 (k9, yo, ssk, k2tog, yo, k9) until 21 sts remain, k9, yo, ssk, k2tog, yo, k8.

Round 2: Knit.

Round 3: K7, yo, ssk, k2, k2tog, yo, k8, (k8, yo, ssk, k2, k2tog, yo, k8) until 21 sts remain, k8, yo, ssk, k2, k2tog, yo, k7.

Round 4: Knit.

Round 5: K10, yo, yo, k11, (k11, yo, yo, k11) until 21 sts remain, k11, yo, yo, k10.

Round 6: K10, knit into the front and back of the double yarnover, k11, (k11, knit into the front and back of the double yarnover, k11) until 23 sts remain, k11, knit into the front and back of the double yarnover, k10.

[-, -, -, -] [-, -, -, -] [-, 406, 406, 430] [430, 430, 430, 430] sts (and 5 steek sts)

Sizes 10 to 13: skip forward to Tiny cats setup.

Increase section nine
(sizes 14+ only)

Round 1: K11, (k10, yo, ssk, k2tog, yo, k10) until 11 sts remain, k11.

Round 2: Knit.

Round 3: K11, (k9, yo, ssk, k2, k2tog, yo, k9) until 11 sts remain, k11.

Round 4: Knit.

Round 5: K11, (k12, yo, yo, k12) until 11 sts remain, k11.

Round 6: K11, (k12, knit into the front and back of the double yarnover, k12) until 11 sts remain, k11.

[-, -, -, -] [-, -, -, -] [-, -, -, -] [-, 464, 464, 464] sts (and 5 steek sts)

Sizes 14 and 15: skip forward to Tiny cats setup.

Increase section ten (size 16 only)

Round 1: K9, yo, ssk, k2tog, yo, k11, (k11, yo, ssk, k2tog, yo, k11) until 24 sts remain, k11, yo, ssk, k2tog, yo, k9.

Round 2: Knit.

Round 3: K8, yo, ssk, k2, k2tog, yo, k10, (k10, yo, ssk, k2, k2tog, yo, k10) until 24 sts remain, k10, yo, ssk, k2, k2tog, yo, k8.

Round 4: Knit.

Round 5: K11, yo, yo, k13, (k13, yo, yo, k13) until 24 sts remain, k13, yo, yo, k11.

Round 6: K11, knit into the front and back of the double yarnover, k13, (k13, knit into the front and back of the double yarnover, k13) until 26 sts remain, k13, knit into the front and back of the double yarnover, k11.

[-, -, -, -] [-, -, -, -] [-, -, -, -] [-, -, -, 500] sts (and 5 steek sts)

Tiny cats setup

Knit five rounds.

Increase round

Work the instruction for your size:

Size 1: K17, (m1, k32) 7 times, m1, k17.

Size 2: Decrease one stitch evenly across round.

Size 3: K11, (m1, k14) 19 times, m1, k11.

Size 4: Increase two stitches across round.

Size 5: K20, (m1, k35) 8 times, m1, k20.

Size 6: K17, (m1, k34) 9 times, m1, k17.

Size 7: K9, (m1, k14) 23 times, m1, k9.

Size 8: K18, (m1, k28) 12 times, m1, k18.

Size 9: K17, (m1, k13) 26 times, m1, k17.

Size 10: K29, m1, k58) 6 times, m1, k29.

Size 11: K14, (m1, k14) 27 times, m1, k14.

Size 12: K20, (m1, k23) 17 times, m1, k19.

Size 13: K14, (m1, k13) 31 times, m1, k13.

Size 14: K16, (m1, k24) 18 times, m1, k16.

Size 15: K8, (m1, k14) 32 times, m1, k8.

Size 16: K21, (m1, k27) 17 times, m1, k20.

[266, 287, 308, 322] [329, 350, 364, 385] [399, 413, 434, 448] [462, 483, 497, 518] (and 5 steek sts)

Eyelets

Switch to CC1.

Round 1: Knit to end.

Round 2: Purl to end.

Round 3: K1, yo, (k2tog, yo) until 1 or 2 sts remain, knit to end.

Round 4: Purl to end.

[267, 288, 309, 323] [330, 351, 365, 386] [400, 414, 435, 449] [463, 484, 498, 519] sts (and 5 steek sts)

Continuing in CC1, knit 4 rounds.

Tiny cats!

Work the **Little cat chart**, starting in the bottom right corner, working right to left, and bringing in CC3 where indicated (see Techniques: Stranded colourwork). Work the marked repeat [38, 41, 44, 46] [47, 50, 52, 55] [57, 59, 62, 64] [66, 69, 71, 74] times.

[305, 329, 353, 369] [377, 401, 417, 441] [457, 473, 497, 513] [529, 553, 569, 593] sts (and 5 steek sts)

Eyelets

Switch to CC1.

Round 1: Knit to end.

Round 2: Purl to end.

Round 3: (K2tog, yo) until 1 st remains, k1.

Round 4: Purl to end.

Short rows

Switch to MC and;

- knit [260, 280, 300, 313] [319, 340, 352, 372] [386, 400, 420, 433] [446, 466, 479, 500] sts, wrap and turn (see Techniques: Short rows),

- purl [215, 231, 247, 257] [261, 279, 287, 303] [315, 327, 343, 353] [363, 379, 389, 407] sts, wrap and turn,

- knit [205, 221, 237, 247] [251, 269, 277, 293] [305, 317, 333, 343] [353, 369, 379, 397] sts, wrap and turn,

- purl [195, 211, 227, 237] [241, 259, 267, 283] [295, 307, 323, 333] [343, 359, 369, 387] sts, wrap and turn,

- and knit to end picking up and securing each wrapped stitch as you come to it.

Knit one round, picking up and securing the remaining wrapped stitches as you reach them.

Final increases/ decreases

Work the instruction for your size:

Sizes 1, 2, 4, 5, 7, 10, 12, 13, and 15 only: Increase [5, 3, -, 3] [3, -, 3, -] [-, 3, -, 5] [3, -, 5, -] stitches across round.

Sizes 3, 6, 8, 9, 11, 14, and 16 only: Decrease one stitch across round.

[310, 332, 352, 372] [380, 400, 420, 440] [456, 476, 496, 518] [532, 552, 574, 592] sts (and 5 steek sts)

Divide for body and sleeves

Slipping stitches purlwise, without knitting;

- move [43, 46, 49, 52] [55, 58, 61, 64] [67, 70, 73, 76] [79, 82, 85, 88] stitches for the front,

- place [68, 72, 76, 80] [78, 82, 86, 90] [92, 96, 100, 104] [106, 110, 114, 118] stitches aside on scrap yarn for the first sleeve,

- move [88, 96, 102, 108] [114, 120, 126, 132] [138, 144, 150, 158] [162, 168, 176, 180] stitches for back,

- place [68, 72, 76, 80] [78, 82, 86, 90] [92, 96, 100, 104] [106, 110, 114, 118] stitches aside on scrap yarn for the second sleeve,

- and move the final [43, 46, 49, 52] [55, 58, 61, 64] [67, 70, 73, 76] [79, 82, 85, 88] stitches for the front.

LITTLE CAT CHART

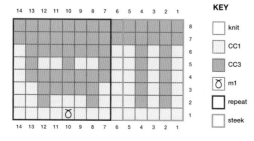

KEY

- knit
- CC1
- CC3
- m1
- repeat
- steek

This time knitting the stitches, knit as far as the set aside sleeves. Cast on [4, 4, 4, 4] [5, 5, 5, 5] [6, 6, 6, 6] [7, 7, 7, 7] stitches using a provisional cast on method (see Techniques: Provisional cast on), place a marker (SM1), cast on another [4, 4, 4, 4] [5, 5, 5, 5] [6, 6, 6, 6] [7, 7, 7, 7] stitches.

Knit across the back of the cardigan until you meet the second set of sleeve stitches, and use a provisional cast on to add [4, 4, 4, 4] [5, 5, 5, 5] [6, 6, 6, 6] [7, 7, 7, 7] stitches, place a marker (SM2), and add another [4, 4, 4, 4] [5, 5, 5, 5] [6, 6, 6, 6] [7, 7, 7, 7] stitches.

[190, 204, 216, 228] [244, 256, 268, 280] [296, 308, 320, 334] [348, 360, 374, 384] sts (and 5 steek sts)

Body

Knit for [8, 8, 8, 8] [7, 7, 7, 7] [6, 6, 5, 5] [5, 5, 5, 5]cm ([3¼, 3¼, 3¼, 3¼] [2¾, 2¾, 2¾, 2¾] [2½, 2½, 2, 2] [2, 2, 2, 2]in) from the underarm.

Waist decreases

Waist decrease round: Knit to 3 sts before SM1, k2tog, k1, slm, k1, ssk, knit to 3 sts before SM2, k2tog, k1, slm, k1, ssk, knit to end.

Work **Waist decrease round** a total of three times, working nine straight rounds between each decrease round.

[178, 192, 204, 216] [232, 244, 256, 268] [284, 296, 308, 322] [336, 348, 362, 372] sts (and 5 steek sts)

Tip: Place a locking marker or bulb pin at every decrease or increase. This makes it very easy to check the total you've worked.

Work straight for [6.5, 6.5, 6, 6] [6, 6, 5.5, 5.5] [5.5, 5.5, 5.5, 5.5] [5, 5, 4.5, 4]cm ([2½, 2½, 2½, 2½] [2½, 2½, 2¼, 2¼] [2¼, 2¼, 2¼, 2¼] [2, 2, 1¾, 1½]in) after the final waist decrease round.

Hip increases

Hip increase round: Knit to 2 sts before SM1, m1, k2, slm, k2, m1, knit to 2 sts before SM2, m1, k2, slm, k2, m1, knit to end.

Work **Hip increase round** a total of six times, working six straight rounds between each increase round.

[202, 216, 228, 240] [256, 268, 280, 292] [308, 320, 332, 346] [360, 372, 386, 396] sts (and 5 steek sts)

Work straight until body measures [33, 33, 32.5, 32.5] [32, 31.5, 31, 30.5] [30.5, 30, 29.5, 29.5] [28.5, 28.5, 28, 27.5]cm ([13¼, 13¼, 13, 13] [12¾, 12½, 12½, 12¼] [12¼, 12, 11¾, 11¾] [11½, 11½, 11¼, 11]in) from the underarm – or until you've reached 2cm (¾in) less than your desired length.

Hem

Eyelets

Switch to CC1.

Round 1: Knit to end.

Round 2: Purl to end.

Round 3: (K2tog, yo) until 2 sts remain, k2.

Round 4: Purl to end.

Switch to MC and knit 5 rounds.

At the end of the last round, bind off the 5 steek stitches (see Techniques: Basic bind off). You will now be working in rows.

[202, 216, 228, 240] [256, 268, 280, 292] [308, 320, 332, 346] [360, 372, 386, 396] sts

Knit one row.

Purl one row.

Picot edge

Switch to CC1.

Picot Edge: (K2tog, yo) until 2 sts remain, k2tog.

[201, 215, 227, 239] [255, 267, 279, 291] [307, 319, 331, 345] [359, 371, 385, 395] sts

Switch to the below-gauge needles.

Work four rows in stocking stitch.

Bind off loosely using the above-gauge needle (see Techniques: Loose bind off).

Sleeve

With the gauge-sized, small-circumference needles, pick up the sleeve stitches from scrap yarn. Pick up the stitches from the provisional cast on and divide them onto your needles so that you're ready to start the round in the centre of the provisionally cast on stitches. Place a marker to indicate the start of round.

[76, 80, 84, 88] [88, 92, 96, 100] [104, 108, 112, 116] [120, 124, 128, 132] sts

Sleeve decreases

With MC, knit [10, 8, 8, 7] [7, 6, 6, 5] [5, 4, 4, 4] [3, 3, 3, 3] rounds.

Sleeve decrease round: K1, k2tog, knit to 3 sts before marker, ssk, k1.

Work **Sleeve decrease round** a total of [12, 14, 15, 16] [16, 17, 18, 19] [20, 21, 22, 23] [25, 26, 26, 26] times, working [10, 8, 7, 6] [6, 6, 5, 5] [4, 4, 4, 3] [3, 3, 3, 3] straight rounds between each decrease round.

[52, 52, 54, 56] [56, 58, 60, 62] [64, 66, 68, 70] [70, 72, 76, 80] sts

Tip: Place a locking marker or bulb pin at every sleeve decrease. This makes it very easy to check the total you've worked.

Knit every round until sleeve measures [42, 41.5, 40.5, 40] [39, 38.5, 37.5, 37] [36.5, 36, 35.5, 35] [34.5, 34, 33.5, 32.5]cm ([16¾, 16½, 16¼, 16] [15½, 15½, 15, 14¾] [14½, 14½, 14¼, 14] [13¾, 13½, 13½, 13]in) from the underarm – or until your sleeves are 2cm (¾in) less than your required length.

Cuff

Eyelets

Switch to CC1.

Round 1: Knit.

Round 2: Purl.

Round 3: (Yo, k2tog) to end.

Round 4: Purl.

Switch to MC and knit 6 rounds.

Picot edge

Switch to CC1.

Picot Edge: (K2tog, yo) to end.

Switch to the below-gauge needles, and work four rounds.

Bind off loosely using the above-gauge needle.

Now work the second sleeve to match.

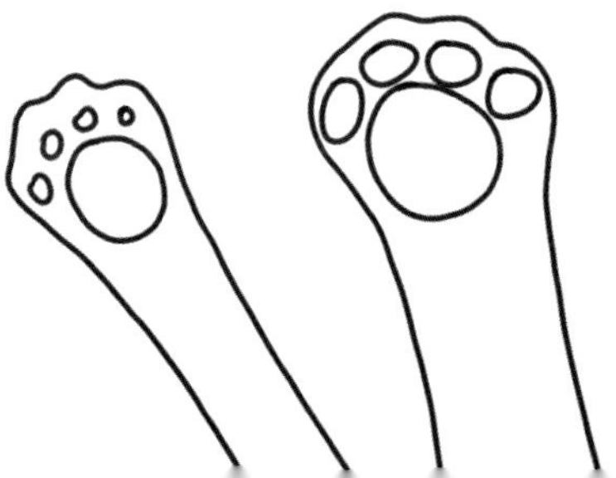

Steeking

Using MC and the crochet hook, reinforce and cut the steek at the centre front of the cardigan (see Techniques: Steeking).

Buttonbands

With CC1 and the gauge-sized needles and working from the top of the left side of the cardigan, starting with the round where you joined for working in the round, and ending with the round where you bound off the steek stitches, pick up and knit three stitches for every four rows (see Techniques: Picking up stitches). The total number of stitches picked should be a multiple of four stitches plus two.

Buttonband row 1 (WS): P2, (k2, p2) to end.

Buttonband row 2 (RS): K2, (p2, k2) to end.

Work **Buttonband rows 1 and 2** three times, then work **Buttonband row 1** once more (seven rows in total), and bind off in pattern (see Techniques: Basic bind off in pattern).

With CC1 and the gauge-sized needles and working from the bottom of the right-hand side of the cardigan, starting with the round where you bound off the steek stitches, and ending with the round where you joined for working in the round, pick up and knit three stitches for every four rows.

The total number of stitches picked should be a multiple of four stitches plus two, and should be the same number of stitches as picked up for the Buttonband.

Work **Buttonband rows 1 and 2** once, then work **Buttonband row 1** once more.

Buttonholes

Plan your button placement, and mark the positions for each buttonhole.

Tip: Use locking markers or bulb pins to mark the buttonhole positions.

On the next row work a three-stitch (or size to fit your chosen buttons) one-row buttonhole (see Techniques: Buttonholes) in the marked positions, working in established pattern between them.

Work **Buttonband rows 1 and 2** once, then work **Buttonband row 1** once more.

Bind off in pattern.

Finishing

Fold the neckline, hem and cuffs at the picot edge, and sew to the underside using CC1 (see Techniques: Turned hems and necklines).

Sew the buttons on, and weave in all ends.

Block to the dimensions shown in the size chart (see Techniques: Blocking).

Toebeans and Tails Shawl

A shawl of simple lace, with a scattering of pawprints, a peeking of cats and a pretty picot edging.

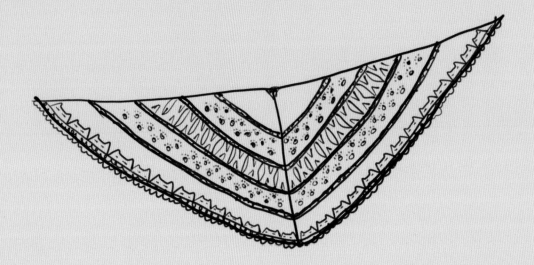

DIMENSIONS

- Width: 150cm (60in).
- Depth: 70cm (28in).

GAUGE

20 sts and 26 rows to 10cm (4in) over stocking stitch worked flat. Wash and gently block your swatch before measuring.

GAUGE ISN'T ESSENTIAL FOR THIS PROJECT, ALTHOUGH VARIATIONS WILL MEAN A LARGER OR SMALLER SHAWL, AND A LOOSER GAUGE MAY REQUIRE MORE YARN.

NEEDLES

- 3.75mm or size needed to obtain gauge: 80cm or longer circular needle.

TOOLS AND NOTIONS

- Stitchmarkers.
- Tapestry needle.

YARN

Eden Cottage Yarns Milburn 4ply: 85% British Bluefaced Leicester, 15% silk; 200m (218yds) per 50g.

- MC: Thyme: 2 balls.
- CC1: Natural: 3 balls.
- CC2: Tea Rose: 2 balls.
- CC3: Catmint: 1 ball.

Notes

Written and charted instructions are included for the lace sections; you can work from either option.

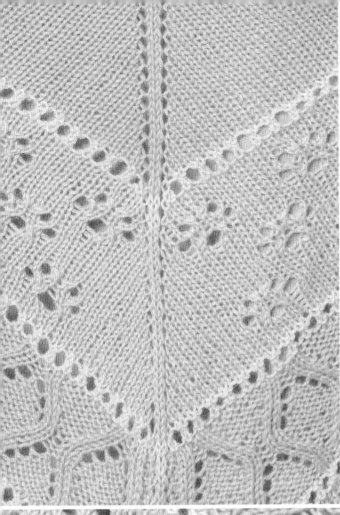

INSTRUCTIONS

A simple start

Using MC, cast on four stitches (see Techniques: Standard cast on).

Row 1: Kyok, k1, place centre marker, k1, kyok. *8 sts*

Row 2: Knit to 1 st before marker, p1, slm, p1, knit to end.

Row 3: K2, kyok, m1o, k1, slm, k1, m1o, kyok, k2. *14 sts*

Row 4: Knit to 1 st before marker, p1, slm, p1, knit to end.

Row 5: K5, place side marker, kyok, m1o, k1, slm, k1, m1o, kyok, place side marker, k5. *20 sts*

Row 6: Knit to 1 st before centre marker, p1, slm, p1, knit to end slipping side markers as you work.

Plain section

Plain row 1 (RS): K5, slm, kyok, knit to 1 st before centre marker, m1o, k1, slm, k1, m1o, knit to 1 st before side marker, kyok, slm, k5.

Plain row 2 (WS): K5, slm, purl to side marker, slipping centre marker as you work, slm, k5.

Work **Plain rows 1 and 2** a total of twenty-three times. *158 sts*

Eyelets

Switch to CC1 and work **Eyelet rows 1 to 4**:

Eyelet row 1 (RS): K5, slm, kyok, knit to 1 st before centre marker (CM), m1o, k1, slm, k1, m1o, knit to one before side marker, kyok, slm, k5.

Eyelet row 2 (WS): K5, slm, knit to 1 st before CM, p1, slm, p1, knit to side marker, slm, k5.

Eyelet row 3 (RS): K5, slm, kyok, (k2tog, yo) to 2 sts before CM, k1, m1o, k1, slm, k1, m1o, k1, (yo, ssk) to 1 st before side marker, kyok, slm, k5.

Eyelet row 4 (WS): K5, slm, knit to 1 st before CM, p1, slm, p1, knit to side marker, slm, k5.

170 sts

Switch to CC2, and work **Plain rows 1 and 2** twice. *182 sts*

TOEBEANS CHART

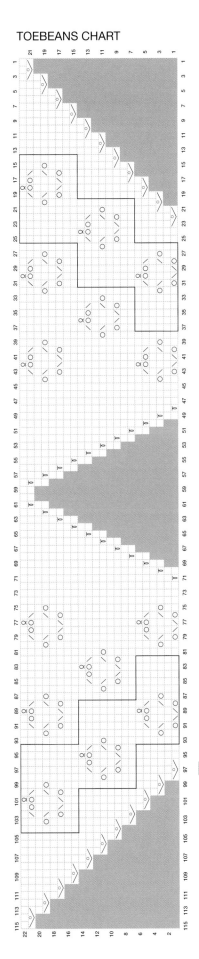

KEY

☐	RS:knit WS:purl
⌣	kyok
○	yo
╱	k2tog
╲	ssk
⊤	m1o
Q	p1 tbl
☐	repeat
▨	no stitch

Toebeans part one

Now work either from the **Toebeans written instructions** or from the **Toebeans chart**.

There's a double yarnover in this section. On the following rounds, make sure that you're working into that twice, and that one of those stitches is through the back loop.

Toebeans written instructions

Row 1 (RS): K5, slm, kyok, k2, (k2, yo, k2tog, ssk, yo, k6) 6 times, k2, yo, k2tog, ssk, yo, k4, m1o, k1, slm, k1, m1o, k4, yo, k2tog, ssk, yo, k2, (k6, yo, k2tog, ssk, yo, k2) 6 times, k2, kyok, slm, k5. *188 sts*

Row 2 (WS): K5, slm, purl to side marker, slm, k5.

Row 3 (RS): K5, slm, kyok, k4, (k1, yo, k2tog, k2, ssk, yo, k5) 6 times, k1, yo, k2tog, k2, ssk, yo, k4, m1o, k1, slm, k1, m1o, k4, yo, k2tog, k2, ssk, yo, k1, (k5, yo, k2tog, k2, ssk, yo, k1) 6 times, k4, kyok, slm, k5. *194 sts*

Row 4 (WS): Repeat **Row 2**.

Row 5 (RS): K5, slm, kyok, k6, (k2, ssk, yo, yo, k2tog, k6) 7 times, m1o, k1, slm, k1, m1o, (k6, yo, yo, k2tog, k2) 7 times, k6, kyok, slm, k5. *200 sts*

Row 6 (WS): K5, slm, p9, (p4, p1 tbl, p7) 7 times, p4, (p7, p1 tbl, p4) 7 times, p9, slm, k5.

Row 7 (RS): K5, slm, kyok, k93, m1o, k1, slm, k1, m1o, k93, kyok, slm, k5. *206 sts*

Row 8 (WS): Repeat **Row 2**.

Row 9 (RS): K5, slm, kyok, k4, (k2, yo, k2tog, ssk, yo, k6) 7 times, k8, m1o, k1, slm, k1, m1o, k8, (k6, yo, k2tog, ssk, yo, k2) 7 times, k4, kyok, slm, k5. *212 sts*

Row 10 (WS): Repeat **Row 2**.

Row 11 (RS): K5, slm, kyok, k6, (k1, yo, k2tog, k2, ssk, yo, k5) 7 times, k9, m1o, k1, slm, k1, m1o, k9, (k5, yo, k2tog, k2, ssk, yo, k1) 7 times, k6, kyok, slm, k5. *218 sts*

Row 12 (WS): Repeat **Row 2**.

Row 13 (RS): K5, slm, kyok, k8, (k2, ssk, yo, yo, k2tog, k6) 7 times, k10, m1o, k1, slm, k1, m1o, k10, (k6, ssk, yo, yo, k2tog, k2) 7 times, k8, kyok, slm, k5. *224 sts*

Row 14 (WS): K5, slm, p11, (p4, p1 tbl, p7) 7 times, p24, (p7, p1 tbl, p4) 7 times, p11, slm, k5.

Row 15 (RS): K5, slm, kyok, k105, m1o, k1, slm, k1, m1o, k105, kyok, slm, k5. *230 sts*

Row 16 (WS): Repeat **Row 2**.

Row 17 (RS): K5, slm, kyok, k6, (k2, yo, k2tog, ssk, yo, k6) 8 times, k6, m1o, k1, slm, k1, m1o, k6, (k6, yo, k2tog, ssk, yo, k2) 8 times, k6, kyok, slm, k5. *236 sts*

Row 18 (WS): Repeat **Row 2**.

Row 19 (RS): K5, slm, kyok, k8, (k1, yo, k2tog, k2, ssk, yo, k5) 8 times, k7, m1o, k1, slm, k1, m1o, k7, (k5, yo, k2tog, k2, ssk, yo, k1) 8 times, k8, kyok, slm, k5. *242 sts*

Row 20 (WS): Repeat **Row 2**.

Row 21 (RS): K5, slm, kyok, k10, (k2, ssk, yo, yo, k2tog, k6) 8 times, k8, m1o, k1, slm, k1, m1o, k8, (k6, ssk, yo, yo, k2tog, k2) 8 times, k10, kyok, slm, k5. *248 sts*

Row 22 (WS): K5, slm, p13, (p4, p1 tbl, p7) 8 times, p20, (p7, p1 tbl, p4) 8 times, p13, slm, k5.

Toebeans chart

Work the **Toebeans chart** starting from the bottom, and reading RS rows from right to left and WS rows from left to right.

Work each chart row as follows: K5, slm, work from chart repeating the marked sections 6 times each (plus the unmarked toes), slm, k5. *248 sts*

Transition

Work **Plain rows 1 and 2** once. *254 sts*

Switch to CC1 and work **Eyelet rows 1 to 4**. *266 sts*

Waving tails

Switch to MC.

Now work either from the **Waving tails written instructions** or from the **Waving tails chart**.

Waving tails written instructions

Row 1 (RS): K5, slm, kyok, k126, m1o, k1, slm, k1, m1o, k126, kyok, slm, k5. *272 sts*

Row 2 (WS): K5, slm, k3, p2, (k1, p2, k7, p2) 10 times, k1, p2, k2, p1, slm, p1, k2, p2, k1, (p2, k7, p2, k1) 10 times, p2, k3, slm, k5.

Row 3 (RS): K5, slm, kyok, p2, k2, (p1, k2, p7, k2) 10 times, p1, k2, p2, m1o, k1, slm, k1, m1o, p2, k2, p1, (k2, p7, k2, p1) 10 times, k2, p2, kyok, slm, k5. *278 sts*

Row 4 (WS): K5, slm, k5, p2, (k1, p2, k7, p2) 10 times, k1, p2, k3, p1, slm, p1, k3, p2, k1, (p2, k7, p2, k1) 10 times, p2, k5, slm, k5.

Row 5 (RS): K5, slm, kyok, p3, k2tog, k1, yo, (p1, yo, k1, ssk, p5, k2tog, k1, yo) 10 times, p1, yo, k1, ssk, p2, m1o, k1, slm, k1, m1o, p2, k2tog, k1, yo, p1, (yo, k1, ssk, p5, k2tog, k1, yo, p1) 10 times, yo, k1, ssk, p3, kyok, slm, k5. *284 sts*

Row 6 (WS): K5, slm, p2, k4, p2, k1, (k2, p2, k5, p2, k1) 10 times, k2, p2, k3, p1, slm, p1, k3, p2, k2, (k1, p2, k5, p2, k2) 10 times, k1, p2, k4, p2, slm, k5.

Row 7 (RS): K5, slm, kyok, k1, p3, k2tog, k1, yo, p1, (p2, yo, k1, ssk, p3, k2tog, k1, yo, p1) 10 times, p2, yo, k1, ssk, p2, m1o, k1, slm, k1, m1o, p2, k2tog, k1, yo, p2, (p1, yo, k1, ssk, p3, k2tog, k1, yo, p2) 10 times, p1, yo, k1, ssk, p3, k1, kyok, slm, k5. *290 sts*

Row 8 (WS): K5, slm, k2, p2, k3, p2, k2, ((k3, p2) twice, k2) 10 times, k3, p2, k3, p1, slm, p1, k3, p2, k3, (k2, (p2, k3) twice) 10 times, k2, p2, k3, p2, k2, slm, k5.

Row 9 (RS): K5, slm, kyok, p1, yo, k1, ssk, p1, k2tog, k1, yo, p2, (p3, yo, k1, ssk, p1, k2tog, k1, yo, p2) 10 times, p3, yo, k1, ssk, p1, k1, m1o, k1, slm, k1, m1o, k1, p1, k2tog, k1, yo, p3, (p2, yo, k1, ssk, p1, k2tog, k1, yo, p3) 10 times, p2, yo, k1, ssk, p1, k2tog, k1, yo, p1, kyok, slm, k5. *296 sts*

Row 10 (WS): K5, slm, k1, (k4, p2, k1, p2, k3) 11 times, k4, p2, k1, p3, slm, p3, k1, p2, k4, (k3, p2, k1, p2, k4) 11 times, k1, slm, k5.

Row 11 (RS): K5, slm, kyok, (p4, k2, p1, k2, p3) 11 times, p4, k2, p1, k2, m1o, k1, slm, k1, m1o, k2, p1, k2, p4, (p3, k2, p1, k2, p4) 11 times, kyok, slm, k5. *302 sts*

Row 12 (WS): K5, slm, k3, (k4, p2, k1, p2, k3) 11 times, k4, p2, k1, p4, slm, p4, k1, p2, k4, (k3, p2, k1, p2, k4) 11 times, k3, slm, k5.

Row 13 (RS): K5, slm, kyok, p2, (p3, k2tog, k1, yo, p1, yo, k1, ssk, p2) 11 times, p3, k2tog, k1, yo, p1, yo, k1, ssk, m1o, k1, slm, k1, m1o, k2tog, k1, yo, p1, yo, k1, ssk, p3, (p2, k2tog, k1, yo, p1, yo, k1, ssk, p3) 11 times, p2, kyok, slm, k5. *308 sts*

Row 14 (WS): K5, slm, k1, p2, k2, ((k3, p2) twice, k2) 11 times, k3, p2, k3, p4, slm, p4, k3, p2, k3, (k2, (p2, k3) twice) 11 times, k2, p2, k1, slm, k5.

Row 15 (RS): K5, slm, kyok, yo, k1, ssk, p1, (p2, k2tog, k1, yo, p3, yo, k1, ssk, p1) 11 times, p2, k2tog, k1, yo, p3, yo, k1, ssk, m1o, k1, slm, k1, m1o, k2tog, k1, yo, p3, yo, k1, ssk, p2, (p1, k2tog, k1, yo, p3, yo, k1, ssk, p2) 11 times, p1, k2tog, k1, yo, kyok, slm, k5. *314 sts*

Row 16 (WS): K5, slm, k4, p2, k1, (k2, p2, k5, p2, k1) 11 times, k2, p2, k5, p4, slm, p4, k5, p2, k2, (k1, p2, k5, p2, k2) 11 times, k1, p2, k4, slm, k5.

Row 17 (RS): K5, slm, kyok, p3, yo, k1, ssk, (p1, k2tog, k1, yo, p5, yo, k1, ssk) 12 times, m1o, k1, slm, k1, m1o, (k2tog, k1, yo, p5, yo, k1, ssk, p1) 12 times, k2tog, k1, yo, p3, kyok, slm, k5. *320 sts*

Row 18 (WS): K5, slm, k7, p2, (k1, p2, k7, p2) 12 times, k1, p1, slm, p1, k1, (p2, k7, p2, k1) 12 times, p2, k7, slm, k5.

Row 19 (RS): K5, slm, kyok, p6, k2, (p1, k2, p7, k2) 12 times, p1, m1o, k1, slm, k1, m1o, p1, (k2, p7, k2, p1) 12 times, k2, p6, kyok, slm, k5. *326 sts*

Row 20 (WS): K5, slm, k9, p2, (k1, p2, k7, p2) 12 times, k2, p1, slm, p1, k2, (p2, k7, p2, k1) 12 times, p2, k9, slm, k5.

Waving tails chart

Work the **Waving tails chart** starting from the bottom, and reading RS rows from right to left and WS rows from left to right.

Work each chart row as follows: K5, slm, work from chart repeating the marked sections 10 times each, slm, k5. *326 sts*

Transition

Switch to CC1 and work **Eyelet rows 1 to 4**. *338 sts*

Switch to CC2 and work **Plain rows 1 and 2** twice. *350 sts*

Toebeans part two

Work the first 14 rows of the **Toebeans written instructions**, (working the repeated sections 13 times on rows 1 to 4, and 14 times on rows 5 to 14), or work **Toebeans chart** rows 1 to 14 (repeating the marked section 13 times). *392 sts*

Transition

Work **Plain rows 1 and 2** once. *398 sts*

Switch to CC1 and work **Eyelet rows 1 to 4**. *410 sts*

Work **Plain rows 1 and 2** 6 times. *446 sts*

WAVING TAILS CHART

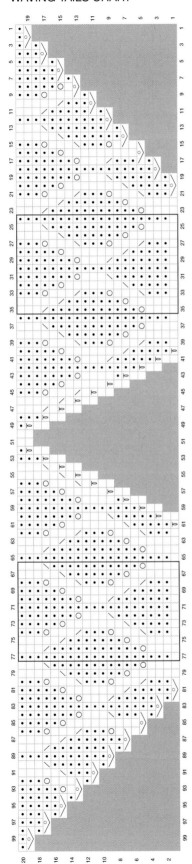

KEY

	RS: knit WS: purl
•	RS: purl WS: knit
	kyok
O	yo
/	k2tog
\	ssk
	m1o
	repeat
	no stitch

LITTLE CAT CHART

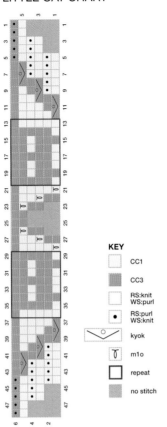

KEY

	CC1
	CC3
	RS:knit WS:purl
•	RS:purl WS:knit
	kyok
	m1o
	repeat
	no stitch

So many tiny cats!

Bringing in CC3 as indicated, work the **Little cat chart**, repeating the marked sections 27 times each (see Techniques: Stranded colourwork). *464 sts*

Keep your colourwork very loose when working the cats.

Transition

Continuing in CC3, work **Plain rows 1 and 2** twice. *476 sts*

Switch to CC1 and work **Eyelet rows 1 to 4**. *488 sts*

Switch to MC and work **Plain rows 1 and 2** twice. *500 sts*

Switch to CC1 and work **Eyelet rows 1 to 4**. *512 sts*

Edging

Switch to CC2.

Edging row: K5, slm, kyok, knit to 1 st before CM, m1o, k1, slm, k1, m1o, knit to 1 st before side marker, kyok, slm, k5. *518 sts*

Bind off using a picot bind off (see Techniques: Picot bind off).

Finishing

Weave in all ends.

Block the shawl. After soaking, stretch the shawl out as much as possible, pinning it into place. Keep the centre spine straight and shape the wings into a shallow v shape (see Techniques: Blocking).

Purrfect Cat Cuffs

These mitts feature frothy lace and peeking cats and are purrfect paw-warmers.

DIMENSIONS

- Size: [Small, Medium].
- To fit palm circumference: [18-21, 22-25]cm ([7¼-8½, 8¾-10]in).

GAUGE

26 sts and 32 rows to 10cm (4in) over stocking stitch worked in the round. Wash and gently block your swatch before measuring.

GAUGE IS ESSENTIAL TO GET THE RIGHT SIZE.

NEEDLES

- 3mm or size needed to obtain gauge: your preferred needles for working a small circumference.

TOOLS AND NOTIONS

- Stitchmarker.
- Tapestry needle.

YARN

Eden Cottage Yarns Milburn 4ply: 85% British Bluefaced Leicester, 15% silk; 200m (218yds) per 50g.
- MC: Tea rose: 1 ball.
- CC1: Natural: 1 ball.
- CC2: Catmint: 1 ball.

INSTRUCTIONS

Cast on

Using MC, and the picot cast on method, cast on [56, 64] stitches (see Techniques: Picot cast on).

Join for working in the round, being careful not to twist the stitches, and place a marker to mark the start of round (see Techniques: Working in the round).

Knit one round.

Eyelets

Switch to CC1.

Eyelet round 1: Knit.

Eyelet round 2: Purl.

Eyelet round 3: (K2tog, yo) to end.

Eyelet round 4: Purl.

Switch to MC.

Next round: K6, place thumb marker 1, knit until 6 sts remain, place thumb marker 2, knit to end.

Thumb shaping

Round 1: Knit to marker, slm, k2 (k2, yo, ssk, k2tog, yo, k2) [5, 6] times, k2, slm, k6.

Round 2: Knit to marker, slm, k2 (k1, yo, ssk, k2, k2tog, yo, k1) [5, 6] times, k2, slm, k6.

Round 3: Knit to marker, slm, k2 (k1, yo, k2tog, k2, ssk, yo, k1) [5, 6] times, k2, slm, k6.

Round 4: Knit to marker, slm, k2 (k2, yo, k2tog, ssk, yo, k2) [5, 6] times, k2, slm, k6.

Round 5: Knit until 2 sts before marker, k2tog, slm, knit to marker, slm, ssk, knit to end.

Work **Rounds 1 to 5** a total of four times. *[48, 56] sts*

Switch to CC1 and work **Eyelet rounds 1 to 4**.

Continuing in CC1, knit four rounds.

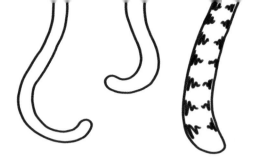

Tiny cats!

Bringing in CC2 as indicated, work the **Little cat chart**, repeating it [6, 7] times across each round (see Techniques: Stranded colourwork).

Switch to CC1 and work **Eyelet rounds 1 to 4**.

Switch to MC and knit four rounds.

Switch to CC1 and work **Eyelet rounds 1 to 4**.

Switch to MC and knit one round.

Continuing in MC, bind off using a picot bind off (see Techniques: Picot bind off).

Finishing

Place a couple of stitches at the end of the first lace edge, between the thumb and fingers.

Weave in ends. Block (see Techniques: Blocking).

Make a second handwarmer to match.

LITTLE CAT CHART

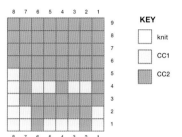

BIG
CATS

Not lions and tigers, quite, but these
giant cats are still fine feline beasts.
They're worked using intarsia.

Kittenface Flippymitts

Colourful cats to warm your paws – with optional little flippy cats to keep your fingers cosy in the cold.

DIMENSIONS

- Size: [Small, Medium].
- To fit palm circumference: [18-20, 21-23]cm ([7¼-8, 8½-9¼]in).

GAUGE

18 sts and 24 rows to 10cm (4in) over stocking stitch. Wash and gently block your swatch before measuring.

GAUGE IS ESSENTIAL TO GET THE RIGHT SIZE.

NEEDLES

- 4.5mm or size needed to obtain gauge: 40cm or longer circular needle, and your preferred needles for working a small circumference.
- 4mm or one size below that needed for gauge: 40cm or longer circular needle.

TOOLS AND NOTIONS

- Stitchmarkers.
- Scrap yarn for holding stitches.
- Tapestry needle.

YARN

Eden Cottage Yarns Bowland Aran: 100% British Bluefaced Leicester; 166m (180yds) per 100g.

- MC: Echinops: 1 skein.
- CC1: Rambing Rose: 1 skein.
- CC2: Bark: 1 skein.
- CC3: Charcoal: 2 metres.

Mitts

Cast on

Using MC and the gauge-sized circular needle, cast on [34, 38] stitches (see Techniques: Standard cast on).

Row 1: (K2, p2) until 2 sts remain, k2.

Row 2: (P2, k2) until 2 sts remain, p2.

Work **Rows 1 and 2** a total of twice.

Work six rows in stocking stitch.

Cats!

Work the **Kitty mitts chart** for your size, bringing in CC1, CC2, and CC3 as indicated (see Techniques: Intarsia).

Thumb increases

Continue working with CC1 and CC2 as established, twisting the yarns around each other at the halfway point.

Row 1: K2, m1, knit until 2 sts remain, m1, k2.

Row 2: P2, m1, purl until 2 sts remain, m1p, p2.

Work **Rows 1 and 2** a total of three times. [46, 50] sts

Size M only: Work **Row 1** once more. [-, 52] sts

All sizes: Work [2, 3] rows in stocking stitch, ending with a WS row.

Thumb decreases

Row 1: K2, ssk, knit until 4 sts remain, k2tog, k2.

Row 2: Purl to end.

Work **Rows 1 and 2** a total of [3, 4] times. [40, 44] sts

Hand decreases

Row 1: K2, ssk, knit to 4 sts before colour change, k2tog, k4, ssk, knit until 4 sts remain, k2tog, k2.

Row 2: Purl to end.

Work **Rows 1 and 2** a total of two times. [32, 36] sts

Knit one row.

Switch to MC, and purl one row.

KITTY MITTS CHART – SMALL

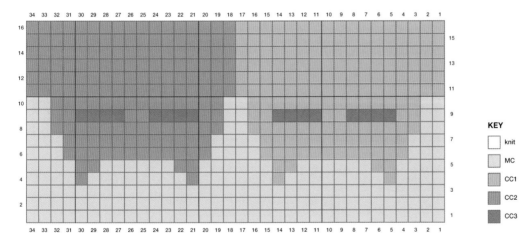

KEY

☐	knit
☐	MC
☐	CC1
☐	CC2
☐	CC3

KITTY MITTS CHART – MEDIUM

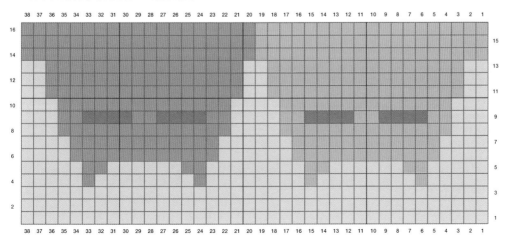

Cuff ribbing

Switch to the below-gauge needles.

Ribbing row 1: K3, (p2, k2) until 1 stitch remains, k1.

Ribbing row 2: P3, (k2, p2) until 1 st remains, p1.

Work **Ribbing rows 1 and 2** a total of four times.

Bind off in pattern using a stretchy bind off method (see Techniques: Stretchy bind off).

Make a second mitt the same as the first one.

Flippy tips (optional)

Cast on

Using CC1 and the gauge-sized small-circumference needles, cast on [36, 40] stitches.

Join for working in the round, being careful not to twist the stitches, and place a marker to mark the start of round (see Techniques: Working in the round).

Edging setup: K[18, 20], pm, k[2, 3], (p2, k2) four times, k[0, 1].

Edging round: Knit to m, slm, k[2, 3], (p2, k2) four times, k[0, 1].

Work **Edging round** a total of three times.

Knit [18, 22] rounds.

Eyes and ears

Eyes: (Ssk, k2, k [4, 5] in CC3, k2, k [4, 5] in CC3, k2, k2tog) twice. *[32, 36] sts*

Ear decreases

Round 1: Knit.

Round 2: Knit.

Round 3: (Ssk, knit to 2 sts before marker, k2tog, slm) twice.

Work **Rounds 1 to 3** a total of two times. *[24, 28] sts*

Ear tip shaping

The ear tips are worked over the four stitches on either side of the marker.

Work the ear tip shaping as follows;

- k4, turn, p8, turn, k4,
- ssk, k2tog, turn, p2tog tbl,
- p2tog, p2tog tbl, turn, k2tog,
- slip last worked stitch to left needle, and ssk it with the final stitch.

Break yarn.

Place the first [4, 6] stitches and the last [4, 6] stitches onto scrap yarn.

Arrange the remaining eight stitches so that you have four stitches on each needle tip ready to start the tip shaping for the other ear.

Rejoin yarn and repeat ear tip shaping for the remaining eight stitches, leaving a long tail when you break the yarn.

Turn inside out and use the long tail to run a couple of stitches along the inside of the ear.

Turn right side out, place the held stitches on two needles, and graft together (see Techniques: Grafting).

Now make a second flippy tip using CC2 in place of CC1.

Finishing

With the right sides together, sew up the side seam of each mitten, leaving a gap along the thumb slant (see Techniques: Side seams).

Sew the non-ribbed edge of the flippy tip to the outside of the back of the mitten.

Weave in all ends, and block (see Techniques: Blocking).

Creepy Catty Capelet

This capelet has some particularly creepy cats glowering out. It's a perfect shoulder-layer for summer evenings, or for layering up a little bit more in colder weather. It's edged with an i-cord for a neat finish.

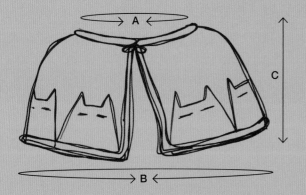

DIMENSIONS

	SIZE 1	SIZE 2	SIZE 3
A: NECKLINE	52cm (20¾in)	59cm (23½in)	66cm (26½in)
B: HEM	150cm (60in)	190cm (76in)	225cm (90in)
C: LENGTH	35cm (14in)	37.5cm (15in)	40cm (16in)

GAUGE

18 sts and 24 rows to 10cm (4in) over stocking stitch worked flat. Wash and block your swatch before measuring.

GAUGE IS ESSENTIAL TO GET THE RIGHT SIZE.

NEEDLES

- 4.5mm or size needed to obtain gauge, 60cm or longer circular needle.

TOOLS AND NOTIONS

- Stitchmarkers.
- Tapestry needle.
- Clasp.

YARN

Eden Cottage Yarns Bowland Aran: 100% British Bluefaced Leicester; 166m (180yds) per 100g.

- MC: Echinops: [2, 3, 3] skeins.
- CC1: Rambing Rose: [1, 2, 2] skeins.
- CC2: Bark:[1, 2, 2] skeins.
- CC3: Charcoal: 1 skein.

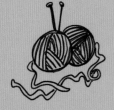

INSTRUCTIONS

Cast on and setup

Using CC1, and the i-cord cast on method, cast on [92, 106, 118] stitches (see Techniques: I-cord cast on).

Switch to MC and purl one row.

Faux-i-cord border setup (RS): Sl1, k1, sl1, k1, p1, place border marker, knit until 5 sts remain, place border marker, p1, k1, sl1, k1, sl1.

Throughout the pattern, work the border stitches as follows:

RS rows: Sl1, k1, sl1, k1, p1, slm, work to border marker, slm, p1, sl1, k1, sl1, k1.

WS rows: Sl1, p1, sl1, p1, k1, slm, work to border marker, slm, k1, sl1, p1, sl1, p1.

Work six rows in stocking stitch (working the border stitches as set).

Increase section one

Inc row 1: Work border, k[3, 2, 2], m1, (k4, m1) to [3, 2, 2] sts before marker, k[3, 2, 2], work border. *[112, 130, 145] sts*

Work three rows in stocking stitch (working the border stitches as set).

Short rows

Work border, sm, and

- knit [86, 100, 113] sts, wrap and turn (see Techniques: Short rows),
- purl [68, 80, 91] sts, wrap and turn,
- knit [64, 76, 87] sts, wrap and turn,
- purl [60, 72, 83] sts, wrap and turn,
- and knit to border marker picking up and securing each wrapped stitch as you come to it, slm, work border.

Next row: Work border, slm, purl to border marker picking up and securing the remaining wrapped stitches as you reach them, slm, work border.

Increase section two

Inc row 2: Work border, slm, k[4, 3, 3], m1, (k5, m1) to [3, 2, 2] sts before marker, k[3, 2, 2], slm, work border. *[132, 154, 172] sts*

Work five rows in stocking stitch.

Increase section three

Inc row 3: Work border, slm, k[4, 3, 3], m1, (k6, m1) to [4, 3, 3] sts before marker, k[4, 3, 3], slm, work border. *[152, 178, 199] sts*

Work five rows in stocking stitch.

Increase section four

Inc row 4: Work border, slm, k[5, 4, 4], m1, (k7, m1) to [4, 3, 3] sts before marker, k[4, 3, 3], slm, work border. *[172, 202, 226] sts*

Work five rows in stocking stitch.

Size one: skip forward to Cat setup.

Increase section five (sizes 2 and 3 only)

Inc row 5: Work border, slm, k[-, 4, 4], m1, (k8, m1) to [-, 4, 4] sts before marker, k[-, 4, 4], slm, work border. *[-, 226, 253] sts*

Work five rows in stocking stitch.

Size two: skip forward to Cat setup.

Increase section six (size 3 only)

Inc row 6: Work border, slm, k[-, -, 5], m1, (k9, m1) to [-, -, 4] sts before marker, k[-, -, 4], slm, work border. *[-, -, 280] sts*

Work five rows in stocking stitch (working the border stitches as set).

Cat setup

Next row: Work border, slm, (kfb, k25, kfb, pm) [6, 8, 10] times, omitting last pm, slm, work border. *[184, 242, 300] sts*

Work five rows in stocking stitch (working the border stitches as set).

Next row: Work border, slm, (kfb, knit to 1 st before marker, kfb, slm) [6, 8, 10] times, work border. *[196, 258, 320] sts*

Creepy cats!

Work the **Creepy cat chart**, repeating it a total of [3, 4, 5] times across each row, starting with a WS row, bringing in CC1, CC2, and CC3, and working the increases as indicated (see Techniques: Intarsia), and continuing to work the border stitches in MC as established. *[220, 290, 360] sts*

CREEPY CAT CHART

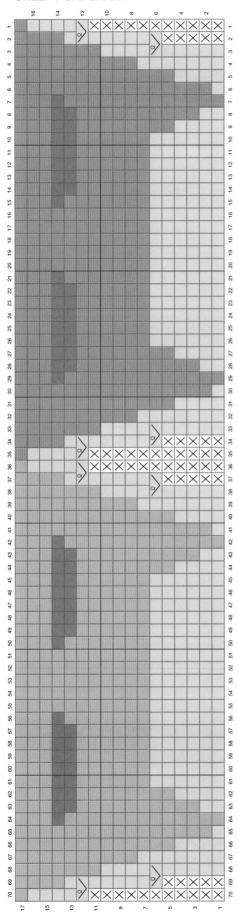

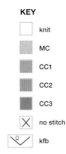

KEY

☐	knit
▨	MC
▨	CC1
▨	CC2
▨	CC3
☒	no stitch
⟨kfb⟩	kfb

Final cape increases

CONTINUE TO WORK THE COLOURS AS ESTABLISHED IN THE CREEPY CAT CHART.

Final increase row: Work border, slm, (kfb, knit to 1 st before marker, kfb, slm) [6, 8, 10] times, work border.

Work **Final increase row** a total of [4, 3, 2] times, working [5, 7, 11] rows in stocking stitch after each increase row and working the border stitches as established. *[268, 338, 400] sts*

I-cord bind off

Bind off using a three-stitch i-cord bind off (see Techniques: I-cord bind off).

Finishing

Weave in all ends. Attach a clasp to just below the neckline.

Block flat, pinning out the hem carefully to discourage curling (see Techniques: Blocking).

Big Cat Cardigan

This loose, long-line cardigan is a perfectly comfy, cosy and catty knit. Pockets are hidden behind the cats.

DIMENSIONS

	SIZE 1	SIZE 2	SIZE 3	SIZE 4	SIZE 5
A: CHEST	80cm (32in)	100cm (40in)	120cm (48in)	140cm (56in)	160cm (64in)
B: LENGTH	75cm (30in)	75cm (30in)	75cm (30in)	75cm (30in)	75cm (30in)
C: SLEEVE LENGTH	52.5cm (21in)	52.5cm (21in)	52.5cm (21in)	52.5cm (21in)	52.5cm (21in)

Sizes are for the completed cardigan. This cardigan is designed to be worn with a bit of positive ease, so choose a size 10-30cm (4-12in) larger than your chest measurement, depending on how loose you'd like the fit.

GAUGE

18 sts and 24 rows to 10cm (4in) over stocking stitch worked flat. Wash and block your swatch before measuring.

GAUGE IS ESSENTIAL TO GET THE RIGHT SIZE.

NEEDLES

- 4.5mm or size needed to obtain gauge: 60cm and 100cm or longer circular needles.
- 2.75mm: 40cm or longer circular needles (for working the pocket stitches).

TOOLS AND NOTIONS

- Stitchmarkers.
- Locking markers or bulb pins – for keeping track of increases and decreases, and marking buttonhole positions.
- Scrap yarn or spare circular needle– for holding stitches.
- Tapestry needle.
- 6 buttons – 25mm (1in) or larger.

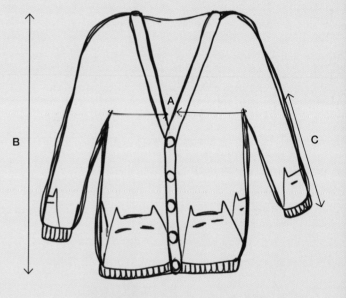

YARN

Eden Cottage Yarns Bowland Aran: 100% British Bluefaced Leicester; 166m (180yds) per 100g.
- MC: Echinops: [6, 7, 8, 9, 10] skeins.
- CC1: Rambing Rose: [2, 2, 3, 3, 3] skeins.
- CC2: Bark: [2, 2, 3, 3, 3] skeins.
- CC3: Charcoal: 1 skein.

You will also need 100m (109yds), about 25g, of any 4-ply or sock weight yarn for the pocket linings.

Notes

Construction

This cardigan is worked top down. The front and back shoulders are started separately, then joined to work the body in one piece. The sleeves are worked separately. Once the cardigan has been sewn up the buttonband is picked up and worked.

Adjustments

For a longer cardigan, you can just work more rows before you start the cat chart – but be aware that the pockets will also be lower. If you'd prefer a longer cardigan without lowering the pockets you can either continue working the cats (each one has their own trajectory) or increase the depth of the hem.

For longer/ shorter arms, add or omit rows before you begin the arm shaping.

This cardigan is designed to be worked with at least 20cm (8in) of positive ease. If you're planning it as a more fitted knit you may want to add a little more length to the sleeves before starting the sleeve decreases.

Back right

Using MC and the gauge-sized needles, cast on [12, 20, 28, 36, 44] stitches (see Techniques: Standard cast on).

Row 1: Knit to end.

Row 2: Purl to end.

Row 3: K1, m1, knit to end.

Row 4: Purl to end.

Row 5: K1, m1, knit to end.

Row 6: Purl to end.

Row 7: K1, m1, knit to end.

Row 8: Purl to 1 st before end, m1, p1.

Row 9: K1, m1, knit to end.

Row 10: Purl to 1 st before end, m1, p1. *[18, 26, 34, 42, 50] sts*

Break yarn and set aside on scrap yarn or a spare circular needle.

Back left

Using MC and the gauge-sized needles, cast on [12, 20, 28, 36, 44] stitches.

Row 1: Knit to end.

Row 2: Purl to end.

Row 3: Knit to 1 st before end, m1, k1.

Row 4: Purl to end.

Row 5: Knit to 1 st before end, m1, k1.

Row 6: Purl to end.

Row 7: Knit to 1 st before end, m1, k1.

Row 8: P1, m1p, purl to end.

Row 9: Knit to 1 st before end, m1, k1.

Row 10: P1, m1, purl to end. *[18, 26, 34, 42, 50] sts*

Don't break the working yarn.

Join back pieces

Move the back right onto your circular needle, at the far side to the working yarn. Make sure the neck sides with the increases are next to each other and that you're looking at the right side of each piece, ready to start the next row.

Knit across the back left, turn work and cast on [28, 30, 32, 34, 36] stitches using the cable cast on method (see Techniques: Cable cast on), turn again and knit across the back right. *[64, 82, 100, 118, 136] sts*

Continue working in stocking stitch until you've completed [48, 52, 56, 60, 64] rows from the original cast on edge.

Break yarn and set aside on scrap yarn or a spare circular needle.

Front right

Using MC and the gauge-sized needles, cast on [12, 20, 28, 36, 44] stitches.

Work in stocking stitch for a total of [26, 24, 22, 20, 18] rows.

Neckline increases

Row 1: Knit to 1 st before end, m1, k1.

Row 2: Purl.

Row 3: Knit.

Row 4: P1, m1, purl to end.

Row 5: Knit.

Row 6: Purl.

Work **Rows 1 to 6** until you've completed [48, 52, 56, 60, 64] rows from cast on edge, and ending with **Row 4**. *[20, 30, 40, 50, 60] sts*

Break yarn and set aside on scrap yarn or a spare circular needle.

Tip: Place a locking marker or bulb pin at every neckline increase. This makes it very easy to check the total you've worked.

Front left

Using MC and the gauge-sized needles, cast on [12, 20, 28, 36, 44] stitches.

Work in stocking stitch for a total of [26, 24, 22, 20, 18] rows.

Neckline increases

Row 1: K1, m1, knit to end.

Row 2: Purl.

Row 3: Knit.

Row 4: Purl to 1 st before end, m1, p1.

Row 5: Knit.

Row 6: Purl.

Work **Rows 1 to 6** until you've completed [48, 52, 56, 60, 64] rows from cast on edge, and ending with **Row 4**. *[20, 30, 40, 50, 60] sts*

Don't break the working yarn.

Join front and back

Move the back and the front right onto the circular needle, taking care to keep the neckline increases at the edge, and the back in the centre. Make sure that the RS is facing you for all three pieces, ready to start the next row with the left front.

Work the joining row as follows;

- knit across the left front,
- turn work and cast on six stitches using the cable cast on method,
- turn and knit across the back,
- turn and cast on six stitches using the cable cast on method,
- turn again and knit across the right front. *[116, 154, 192, 230, 268] sts*

Purl one row.

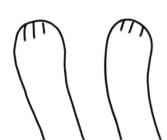

Neckline increases (continued)

Row 1: K1, m1, knit to 1 st before end, m1, k1.

Row 2: Purl.

Row 3: Knit.

Row 4: P1, m1, purl to 1 st before end, m1, p1.

Row 5: Knit.

Row 6: Purl.

Work **Rows 1 to 6** until you've increased a total of [20, 21, 22, 23, 22] stitches on each side of the cardigan, including the increases that happened before joining the back and front. *[140, 176, 212, 248, 284] sts*

Work in stocking stitch until the cardigan measures 49cm (19½in) from the top of the shoulder and ending with a RS row.

Some very big cats!

Work across **Big cat charts A, [B1, B2, B3, B4, B5] and C**, starting with a WS row, and bringing in CC1, CC2, and CC3 as indicated (see Techniques: Intarsia).

START AT THE BOTTOM OF THE CHART. ON WS ROWS WORK EACH ROW FROM LEFT TO RIGHT ACROSS ALL THREE CHARTS (CHART A, THEN THE B CHART FOR YOUR SIZE, AND THEN CHART C). ON RS ROWS WORK EACH ROW FROM RIGHT TO LEFT ACROSS ALL THREE CHARTS (CHART C, THEN B, THEN A).

Work the first five rows of the Big cat charts.

On Row 6 (a RS row) of the Big Cat charts work the chart until you reach the marked pocket stitches. You will now work on just these stitches to make the pocket lining.

Pocket instructions

Work the 17 marked pocket stitches back and forth as follows:

Pocket row 1: Knit.

Pocket row 2: Purl.

Pocket row 3: Knit.

Pocket row 4: Purl.

Pocket row 5: Kfb, knit to 1 st before end, kfb. *19 pocket sts*

Pocket row 6: Purl. Break MC.

Switch to the small needles and the pocket yarn.

BIG CATS CHART A

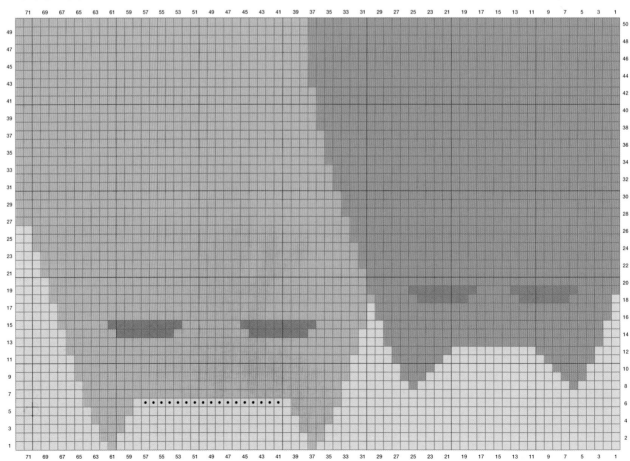

BIG CATS CHART B1

BIG CATS CHART B2

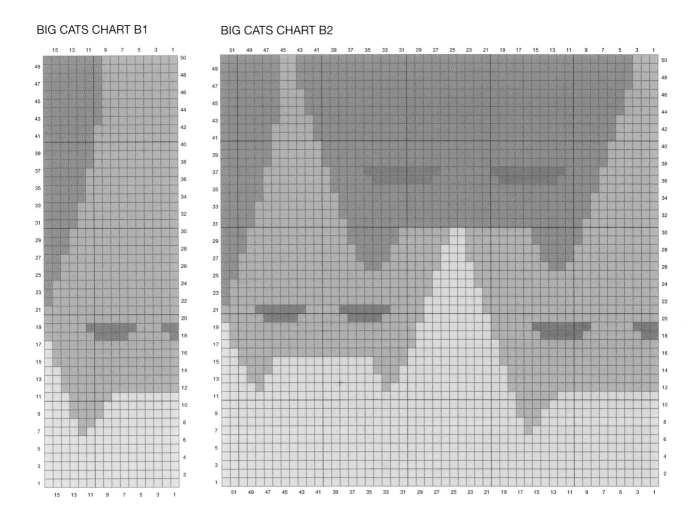

BIG CATS CHART B3

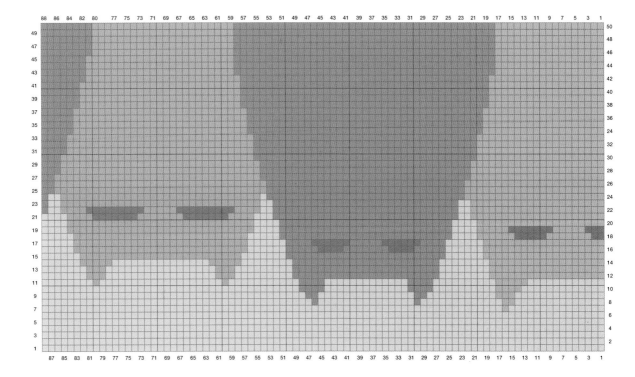

KEY

- knit
- MC
- CC1
- CC2
- CC3
- • pocket

BIG CATS CHART B4

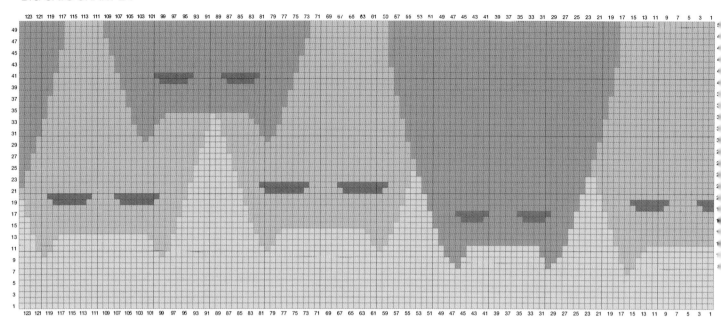

BIG CATS CHART B5

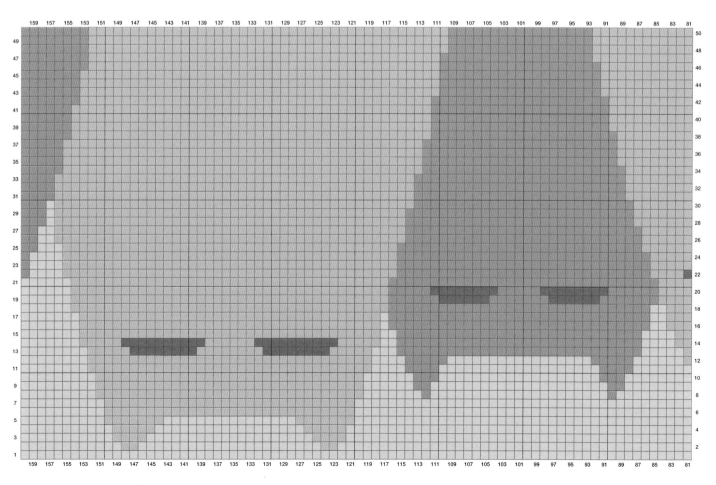

BIG CATS CHART C

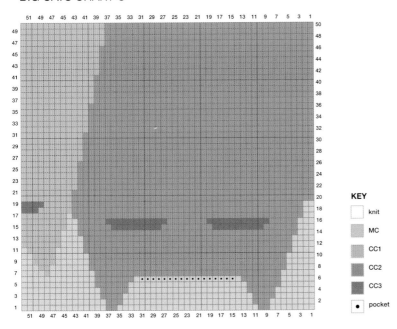

KEY

	knit
	MC
	CC1
	CC2
	CC3
•	pocket

Pocket lining setup: Kfb, (k1, kfb) to end. *29 pocket sts*

Work these 29 sts in stocking stitch, starting with a purl row, for 24cm (9½in), and ending with a knit row. Break pocket yarn.

Switch to the gauge-sized needles and MC.

Pocket row 7: P2tog, (p1, p2tog) to end. *19 pocket sts*

Pocket row 8: K2tog, knit until 2 sts remain, ssk. *17 pocket sts*

Pocket row 9: Purl.

Pocket row 10: Purl.

Continue working row 6 of the Big Cat charts to the next marked pocket, and repeat **Pocket instructions**.

Complete row 6 of the Big cat charts and work the remaining rows of the charts.

Continuing in MC, purl one row.

BIG CATS CHART B5 (CONTINUED)

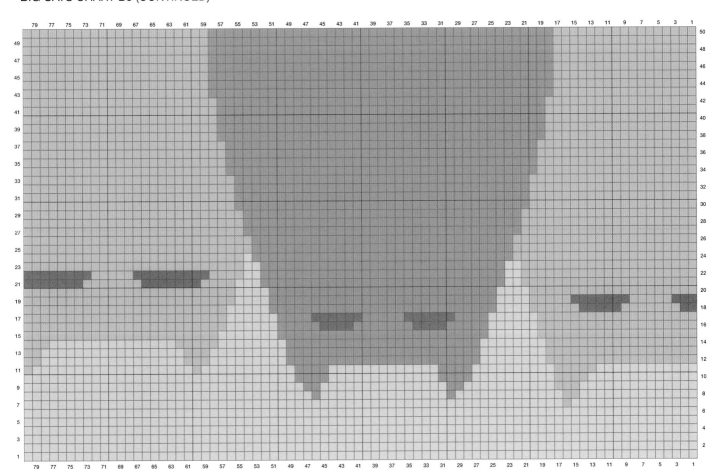

Ribbing

Ribbing row 1: K3, (p2, k2) until one st remains. k1.

Ribbing row 2: P3, (k2, p2) until 1 st remains, p1.

Work five repeats of **Ribbing rows 1 and 2**, then bind off in pattern (see Techniques: Basic bind off in pattern).

Sleeves

Using MC and the gauge-sized needles, cast on [74, 80, 84, 92, 96] stitches and work for [18, 12, 12, 18, 18] rows in stocking stitch, beginning with a RS row.

Sleeve decreases

The sleeve chart starts before the sleeve shaping is completed.

RS decrease row: K1, ssk, knit until 3 sts remain, k2tog, k1.

WS decrease row: P1, p2tog tbl, purl until 3 sts remain, p2tog, p1.

*Begin sleeve shaping with a **RS decrease row**.*

Work a total of [16, 17, 17, 19, 19] sleeve decreases, working [5, 5, 5, 4, 4] rows between them, and working the **RS decrease row** or **WS decrease row** as appropriate.

Tip: Place a locking marker or bulb pin at every sleeve decrease. This makes it very easy to check the total you've worked.

Sleeve cats!

At the same time, after you've worked 66 sleeve rows, begin the **Big cat sleeve chart**, starting with a RS row, bringing in CC1, CC2, and CC3 as indicated. *[58, 62, 66, 72, 76] sts*

Sleeve chart setup: K [0, 2, 4, 7, 9], pm, work row 1 of chart, pm, k [0, 2, 4, 7, 9].

Continue working the sleeve decreases alongside the sleeve chart, adding one stitch of CC1 and CC2 every three rows, as set, until there's no longer any MC at the edges.

Complete the 50 rows of the Big cat sleeve chart. Switch to MC and purl one row. *[42, 46, 50, 54, 58] sts*

Cuff ribbing

Ribbing row 1: K2, (p2, k2) to end.

Ribbing row 2: P2, (k2, p2) to end.

Work five repeats of **Ribbing rows 1 and 2**, then bind off in pattern.

Now work the second sleeve to match.

BIG CATS SLEEVE CHART

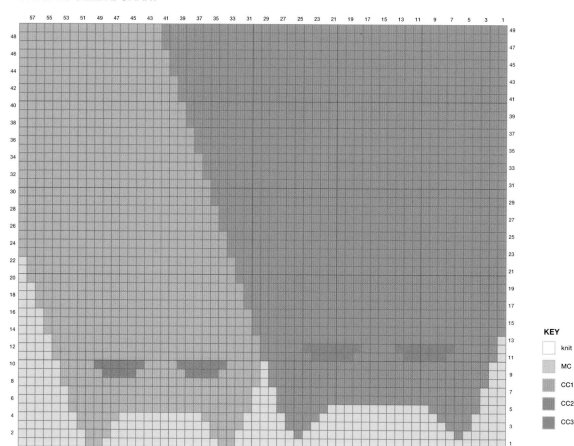

KEY

⬜	knit
▨	MC
▨	CC1
▨	CC2
▨	CC3

Making up

Sew up the shoulders of the cardigan (see Techniques: Shoulder seams), seam the sleeves (leaving the four rows at the top unseamed), and attach the sleeves to the cardigan, with the four loose rows sewn to the underarm stitches (see Techniques: Side seams).

Buttonband and neckline

Using MC, and the longest circular needle, starting at the bottom right hand side, pick up and knit three stitches for every four rows along the sides, and one stitch for every stitch column across the back neck (see Techniques: Picking up stitches). The total number of stitches picked up should be a multiple of four stitches plus two.

You'll start the buttonband on the WS of the knitting.

Buttonband row 1: P2, (k2, p2) to end.

Buttonband row 2: K2, (p2, k2) to end.

Work **Buttonband rows 1 and 2** twice (four rows).

Buttonholes

Plan your button placement on the next row – place five or six buttons evenly across the section of buttonband below the neckline, and mark the position of each buttonhole on the opposite band.

Tip: Use locking markers or bulb pins to mark the buttonhole positions.

On the next row work a four-stitch (or size to fit your chosen buttons) one-row buttonhole (see Techniques: Buttonholes) in the marked positions, working in established pattern between them.

Work **Buttonband row 2**, and then another two repeats (four rows) of **Buttonband rows 1 and 2**.

Bind off in pattern.

Finishing

Seam up the sides of the pockets (see Techniques: Side seams).

Sew the buttons on, and weave in all ends.

Block to the dimensions shown in the diagram (see Techniques: Blocking).

Peeky Pompom Cat Hat

A foursome of creepy cats glower out over the brim of this cosy hat.

DIMENSIONS

- Size: [Small, Medium].
- To fit head circumference: [47-53, 54-60]cm ([18¾-21¼, 21½-24]in). This hat is designed to be worn with at least 2.5cm (1in) stretch at the brim.

GAUGE

18 sts and 24 rows to 10cm (4in) over stocking stitch worked in the round. Wash and gently block your swatch before measuring.

GAUGE IS ESSENTIAL FOR
A WELL-FITTING HAT.

NEEDLES

- 4.5mm or size needed to obtain gauge: 40cm or longer circular needle or pair of straight needles.
- 4mm or one size below that needed for gauge: 40cm or longer circular needle or pair of straight needles.

TOOLS AND NOTIONS

- Tapestry needle.

YARN

Eden Cottage Yarns Bowland Aran: 100% British Bluefaced Leicester; 166m (180yds) per 100g.

- MC: Echinops: 1 skein.
- CC1: Rambing Rose: 1 skein.
- CC2: Bark: 1 skein.
- CC3: Charcoal: 2 metres.

INSTRUCTIONS

Cast on

Using MC, and the gauge-sized needles, cast on nine stitches (see Techniques: Standard cast on).

Crown shaping

Row 1 (RS): (K1, m1) until 1 st remains, k1. *17 sts*

Row 2 (WS): Purl to end.

Row 3 (RS): K1, (kyok, k3) to end. *25 sts*

Row 4 (WS): Work as **Row 2**.

Row 5 (RS): K3, (kyok, k5) until 4 sts remain, kyok, k3. *33 sts*

Row 6 (WS): Work as **Row 2**.

Row 7 (RS): K4, (kyok, k7) until 5 sts remain, kyok, k4. *41 sts*

Row 8 (WS): Work as **Row 2**.

Row 9 (RS): K5, (kyok, k9) until 6 sts remain, kyok, k5. *49 sts*

Row 10 (WS): Work as **Row 2**.

Row 11 (RS): K6, (kyok, k11) until 7 sts remain, kyok, k6. *57 sts*

Row 12 (WS): Work as **Row 2**.

Row 13 (RS): K7, (kyok, k13) until 8 sts remain, kyok, k7. *65 sts*

Row 14 (WS): Work as **Row 2**.

Row 15 (RS): K8, (kyok, k15) until 9 sts remain, kyok, k8. *73 sts*

Row 16 (WS): Work as **Row 2**.

Row 17 (RS): K9, (kyok, k17) until 10 sts remain, kyok, k9. *81 sts*

Size M only

Row 18 (WS): Work as **Row 2**.

Row 19 (RS): K10, (kyok, k19) until 11 sts remain, kyok, k10. *89 sts*

Both sizes

Work in stocking stitch for a further [8, 10] rows, ending with a RS row.

Peeky cats!

Work the **Peeky cat chart** for your size, starting at the bottom, working from the left on WS rows, and from the right for RS rows, and bringing in CC1, CC2, and CC3 as indicated (see Techniques: Intarsia)

THE PEEKY CAT CHART STARTS WITH A WS ROW.

After completing the Peeky cat chart, work a further 4 rows in CC1, again ending with a RS row.

Brim

Switch to the below-gauge needles.

Ribbing row 1: (P2, k2) until 1 st remains, p1.

Ribbing row 2: K1, (p2, k2) to end.

Work **Ribbing rows 1 and 2** a total of five times.

Bind off in pattern using a stretchy bind-off method (see Techniques: Stretchy bind off).

KEY

	knit
	MC
	CC1
	CC2
	CC3

PEEKY CAT CHART – SMALL

PEEKY CAT CHART – MEDIUM

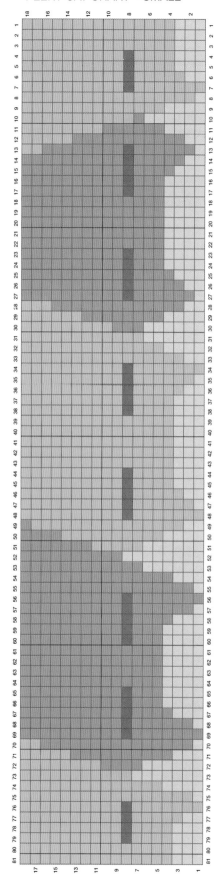

Finishing

Weave in all ends. With the right sides facing each other, seam up the edges of the hat (see Techniques: Side seams).

Turn the brim so that the cats are peeking out from under it, and block to the dimensions given (see Techniques: Blocking).

Use the remaining CC2 to make a pompom and attach it to the crown of the hat (see Techniques: Pompoms).

COOL CATS

Bold, contemporary knits,
with striped rows of cats
glowering out at the world.
These knits combine
stranded colourwork with
simple, classic shapes.

Cropped Catsweater

This is a lovely sweater for layering over longer tops or shirts; it's cropped, wide, and swishy.

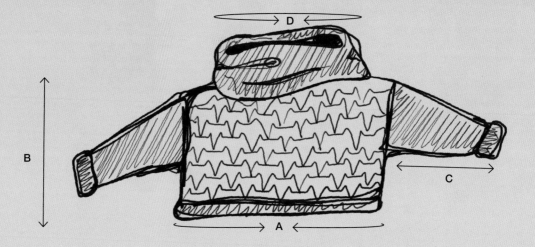

DIMENSIONS

	SIZE 1	SIZE 2	SIZE 3	SIZE 4	SIZE 5
A: CHEST	100cm (40in)	120cm (48in)	140cm (56in)	160cm (64in)	180cm (72in)
B: LENGTH	44cm (17½in)	44cm (17½in)	44cm (17½in)	44cm (1 ½in)	44cm (17½in)
C: SLEEVE LENGTH	41cm (16½in)	40cm (16in)	39cm (15½in)	38cm (15¼in)	37cm (14¾in)
D: NECKLINE	60cm (24in)	64cm (25½in)	64cm (25½in)	68cm (27¼in)	68cm (27¾in)

This sweater is designed to be worn with 20-50cm (8-20in) positive ease.

GAUGE

22 sts and 28 rows to 10cm (4in) over colourwork pattern and in stocking stitch worked in the round. Wash and gently block your swatch before measuring.

GAUGE IS ESSENTIAL TO GET THE RIGHT SIZE.

NEEDLES

- 4mm or size needed to obtain gauge: 40cm and 80cm circular needles, and your preferred needles for working a small circumference.
- 3.75mm or one size below that needed for gauge: 80cm circular needle, and your preferred needles for working a small circumference.
- 4.5mm or one size above that needed for gauge: for binding off.

TOOLS AND NOTIONS

- Stitchmarkers.
- Locking markers or bulb pins – for keeping track of sleeve decreases.
- Scrap yarn or spare circular needle – for holding stitches.
- A crochet hook: a size or two smaller than your gauge needle size – for reinforcing the steeks.
- Small, sharp scissors for steeking.
- Tapestry needle

YARN

Eden Cottage Yarns Milburn DK: 85% British Bluefaced Leicester, 15% silk; 112m (122yds) per 50g.

- MC: Charcoal: [9, 10, 11, 12, 13] balls
- CC1: Steel: 2 balls
- CC2: Rain: 2 balls
- CC3: Catmint: 2 balls

You will also need 10m (11yds) of 4ply weight, non-superwash wool for reinforcing the steeks.

Notes

Construction

The shoulders of the sweater are knit separately, then joined for working in the round for the colourwork cats. After the armholes are steeked, the shoulders are seamed, and sleeves picked up and knit. It's finished with a wide cowl neckline.

Adjustments

If you prefer a less cropped sweater you can work one (or more) extra rows of cats. This will, of course, require extra yarn.

INSTRUCTIONS

Right half of sweater

Using MC, and the gauge-sized needles, cast on [51, 71, 95, 107, 131] stitches using the cable cast on method (see Techniques: Cable cast on).

K [23, 33, 45, 51, 63], place steek marker, k5, place steek marker, knit to end.

Purl one row.

Neck shaping

Row 1: Kfb, knit until 1 st remains, kfb.

Row 2: Purl until 1 st remains, pfb.

Work **Rows 1 and 2** three times, for a total of six rows. *[60, 80, 104, 116, 140] sts*

Break yarn and set aside on scrap yarn or a spare circular needle.

Left half of sweater

Using MC, and the gauge-sized needles, cast on [51, 71, 95, 107, 131] stitches using the cable cast on method.

K [23, 33, 45, 51, 63], place steek marker, k5, place steek marker, knit to end.

Purl one row.

Neck shaping

Row 1: Kfb, knit until 1 st remains, kfb.

Row 2: Pfb, purl to end.

Work **Rows 1 and 2** three times, for a total of six rows. *[60, 80, 104, 116, 140] sts*

Don't break the working yarn.

Join left and right

Join at back

Move the right half of sweater onto your circular needle, at the far end to the working yarn. Make sure that the RS is facing you for both pieces, ready to start the next row with the left half.

Work the joining row as follows;

- kfb, knit to end of left half,
- turn work and cast on [55, 59, 59, 63, 63] stitches using the cable cast on method,
- then turn again and knit across the right half until 1 st remains, kfb. *[177, 221, 269, 297, 345] sts*

Front shaping

Row 1 (WS): Pfb, purl until 1 st remains, pfb.

Row 2 (RS): Kfb, knit until 1 st remains, kfb.

Work **Rows 1 and 2** four times, for a total of eight rows. *[193, 237, 285, 313, 361] sts*

Join at front

Cast on [43, 47, 47, 51, 51] stitches using the cable cast on method, and join for working in the round. *[236, 284, 332, 364, 412] sts*

Knit to first steek marker; this will now be the start of round marker.

Knit one round.

COOL CATS CHART 1

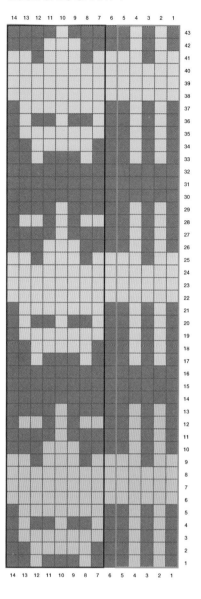

COOL CATS CHART 2

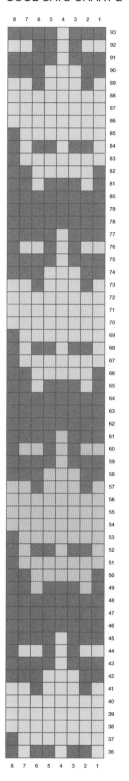

KEY

☐	knit
■	MC
▨	CC1
▨	CC2
☐	CC3
☐	repeat
☐	steek

Cats!

The Cat Chart is in two parts: Progress from working from Cat Chart 1 to working from Cat Chart 2 on the row specified for your size.

Cool cats chart 1

Work each round of the **Cool cats chart 1** as follows: (work the steek stitches, slm, work stitch 6 once, then repeat sts 7 to 14 to the next marker, slm) twice (see Techniques: Stranded colourwork).

Continue working from Cool cats chart 1 until you've completed round [34, 36, 38, 40, 42].

Switch charts

Work round [35, 37, 39, 41, 43] as follows;

- remove start of round marker, bind off five steek stitches (see Techniques: Basic bind off), remove steek marker,
- pass the last stitch before the bound off steek stitches over the stitch remaining on the right needle after the bind off and replace the start of round marker,
- work in pattern to the next steek marker,
- remove steek marker, bind off five steek stitches, remove next steek marker,
- pass the last stitch before the bound off steek stitches over the stitch remaining on the right needle after the bind off,
- work in pattern to end of round. *[224, 272, 320, 352, 400] sts*

Cool cats chart 2

Switch to working from **Cool cats chart 2**, beginning with row [36, 38, 40, 42, 44].

Continue until you've completed this chart.

Hem

Continuing with MC, knit 12 rounds,

Purl one round.

Switch to the below-gauge needles and knit another nine rounds.

Bind off loosely using the above-gauge needle (see Techniques: Loose bind off).

Sleeves

Steek the armholes

Using the crochet hook and steek yarn, reinforce and cut the steek at each armhole (see techniques: Steeking).

Seam the shoulders

Line the shoulder seams up with the stitches matching and seam the front to the back (see techniques: Shoulder seams).

Pick up stitches for sleeves

With the gauge-sized small-circumference needles pick up and knit [78, 81, 84, 87, 90] stitches around the armhole between the body stitches and the steek stitches (see Techniques: Picking up stitches). Begin at the base of the armhole. Pick up three stitches for every four rows, with the extra around the bottom of the armhole. Place a marker to indicate the start of round.

Sleeve decreases

Knit [5, 5, 4, 4, 4] rounds.

Sleeve decrease round: K1, ssk, knit to 3 sts before marker, k2tog, k1.

Work **Sleeve decrease round** a total of 15 times, working [5, 5, 4, 4, 4] straight rounds between each decrease round. *[48, 51, 54, 57, 60] sts*

Tip: Place a locking marker or bulb pin at every sleeve decrease. This makes it very easy to check the total you've worked.

Work straight until sleeve measures [41, 40, 39, 38, 37]cm [16½, 16, 15½, 15¼, 14¾]in from top of sleeve, or until it's the desired length.

Cuffs

Purl one round.

Switch to the below-gauge small-circumference needles and knit another nine rounds.

Bind off loosely using the above-gauge needle.

Now work the second sleeve to match.

Cowl neck

Using the 40cm gauge-sized needle, pick up and knit [132, 140, 140, 148, 148] sts around the neckline, beginning at the centre back. You should be picking up one stitch for each stitch column.

Place a marker to indicate the start of round.

Work in stocking stitch for 20cm (8in).

Bind off loosely using the above-gauge needle.

Finishing

Fold the hem and the cuffs over at the purled row – they should fold naturally at that point – and stitch to the inside of the hem or cuff (see Techniques: Turned hems and necklines).

Fold the cowl back and stitch the bound off edge to the ridge left after you've picked stitches up.

Weave in all ends.

Block to the dimensions in the size table (see Techniques: Blocking). Fold the cowl neck loosely over at about 2.5cm (1in) from the inside edge, and don't press the cowl fabric flat.

Covered in Cats Cowl

These cats will keep you cosy – the cowl is double layered, so it's warm and snug. It's also an excellent way to dip your toes into colourwork.

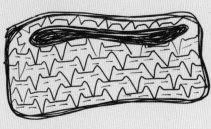

DIMENSIONS

- Circumference: 65cm (26in).
- Depth: 17cm (6¾in).

GAUGE

22 sts and 28 rows to 10cm (4in) over colourwork pattern worked in the round. Wash and gently block your swatch before measuring.

GAUGE ISN'T ESSENTIAL FOR THIS PROJECT, ALTHOUGH VARIATIONS WILL MEAN A LARGER OR SMALLER COWL, AND A LOOSER GAUGE MAY REQUIRE MORE YARN.

NEEDLES

- 4mm or size needed to obtain gauge: 40cm circular needle.
- A second 4mm needle of any length.

TOOLS AND NOTIONS

- One stitchmarker.
- Crochet hook for the provisional cast on.
- Scrap yarn – for provisional cast on.
- A tapestry needle.

YARN

Eden Cottage Yarns Milburn DK: 85% British Bluefaced Leicester, 15% silk; 112m (122yds) per 50g.

- MC: Charcoal: 2 balls.
- CC1: Thyme: 1 ball.
- CC2: Catmint: 1 ball.

INSTRUCTIONS

Cast on and setup

Using scrap yarn and a provisional cast on method, cast on 144 stitches (see Techniques: Provisional cast on).

Join for working in the round, being careful to not twist, and place a marker to mark the start of round (see Techniques: Working in the round).

Knit one round in MC.

Cats are here!

Work the **Cool cats chart** starting from the bottom and working from right to left introducing and breaking CC1 and CC2 as needed (see Techniques: Stranded colourwork). Work the marked repeat 17 times across the round.

Work a total of three repeats of the chart omitting the final two plain rounds in the last repeat.

Finishing

Don't cut the working (MC) yarn yet, but weave in all other ends to the back of the knitting.

Remove the scrap yarn and pick up the provisionally cast on stitches onto the second circular needle.

Cut working (MC) yarn, leaving a very long tail (a little more than three times the circumference of the cowl).

Graft the two ends together, with the right side on the outside (see Techniques: Grafting).

Block (see Techniques: Blocking).

COOL CATS CHART

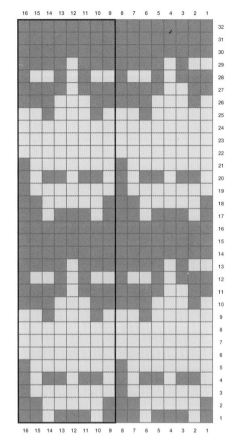

KEY

- ☐ knit
- ■ MC
- ▨ CC1
- ▨ CC2
- ☐ repeat

Slouchy Cat Hat

Wear this hat with a turned brim for a snugger fit, or leave the brim unfolded for the full slouchy cat hat experience.

DIMENSIONS

- Size: [Small, Medium].
- To fit head circumference: [47-53, 54-60]cm ([18¾-21¼, 21½-24]in).

This hat is designed to be worn with at least 2.5cm (1in) stretch at the brim.

GAUGE

22 sts and 28 rows to 10cm (4in) over colourwork pattern worked in the round. Wash and gently block your swatch before measuring.

GAUGE IS ESSENTIAL FOR A WELL-FITTING HAT.

NEEDLES

- 4mm or size needed to obtain gauge: 40cm circular needle and your preferred needles for working a small circumference.
- 3.75mm or one size below than needed for gauge: 40cm circular needle.

TOOLS AND NOTIONS

- Stitchmarkers.
- Tapestry needle.

YARN

Eden Cottage Yarns Milburn DK: 85% British Bluefaced Leicester, 15% silk; 112m (122yds) per 50g.

- MC: Charcoal: [1, 2] balls.
- CC1: Steel: 1 ball.
- CC2: Rain: 1 ball.

INSTRUCTIONS

Cast on and setup

Using MC, and small-circumference needles, cast on 8 stitches (see Techniques: Standard cast on).

Join for working in the round, being careful not to twist the stitches, and place a marker to mark the start of round (see Techniques: Working in the round).

Round 1: Knit.

Round 2: (K1, m1) to end. *16 sts*

Round 3: (K2, pm) until 2 sts remain, k2.

YOU SHOULD NOW HAVE SEVEN CROWN INCREASE MARKERS AND ONE START OF ROUND MARKER.

Crown shaping: part one

Round 1: (Knit to marker, m1, slm) to end.

Round 2: Knit.

Work **Rounds 1 and 2** a total of [10, 12] times. *[96, 112] sts*

Crown shaping: part two

Round 1: Knit.

Round 2: (Knit to marker, m1, slm) to end.

Round 3: Knit.

Work **Rounds 1 to 3** a total of 2 times. On the final knit round remove the seven crown increase markers as you reach them, leaving the start of round marker in place. *[112, 128] sts*

Cats on a hat!

Switch to the 40cm gauge-sized circular needles.

Work the Cool Cats chart, starting from the bottom right, and working the marked repeat a total of [13, 15] times (see Techniques: Stranded colourwork).

Break CC1 and CC2.

Brim

With MC knit 2 rounds.

Next round: (Ssk, k [12, 14]) to end. *[104, 120] sts*

Knit 2 rounds.

Next round: (Ssk, k [11, 13]) to end. *[96, 112] sts*

Switch to CC1, and the below-gauge needles, and knit one round.

Ribbing round: (K2, p2) to end.

Work **Ribbing round** a total of 12 times.

Bind off in pattern, using a stretchy bind off method (see Techniques: Stretchy bind off).

Finishing

Weave in ends, and block (see Techniques: Blocking).

Use the remaining CC1 to make a pompom, and attach it to the tip of the crown (see Techniques: Pompoms). Mix in a little of CC2 and MC for a speckled pompom, if you like!

COOL CATS CHART

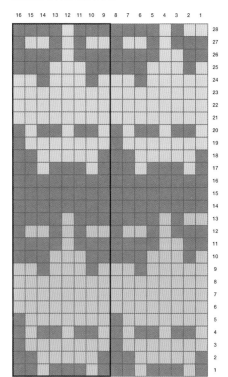

KEY

- knit
- MC
- CC1
- CC2
- repeat

Kitten Mittens

Keep your paws cosy in these classic, colourwork mittens.

DIMENSIONS

- Size: [Small, Medium].
- To fit palm circumference: [18-21, 22-25]cm ([7¼-8½, 8¾-10]in).

GAUGE

22 sts and 28 rows to 10cm (4in) over colourwork pattern worked in the round. Wash and gently block your swatch before measuring.

GAUGE IS ESSENTIAL TO GET THE RIGHT SIZE.

NEEDLES

- 4mm or size needed to obtain gauge: your preferred needles for working a small circumference.
- 3.75mm or one size smaller than needed for gauge: your preferred needles for working a small circumference.

TOOLS AND NOTIONS

- Stitchmarkers.
- Scrap yarn or spare circular needle–for holding stitches.
- Tapestry needle.

YARN

Eden Cottage Yarns Milburn DK: 85% British Bluefaced Leicester, 15% silk; 112m (122yds) per 50g.

- MC: Charcoal: 2 balls.
- CC1: Steel: 1 ball.
- CC2: Rain: 1 ball.

INSTRUCTIONS

Thumb

Using MC, and the gauge-sized needles cast on [4, 5] stitches (see Techniques: Standard cast on).

Join for working in the round, being careful not to twist the stitches, and place a marker to mark the start of round (see Techniques: Working in the round).

Round 1: Kfb to end. *[8, 10] sts*

Round 2: Kfb to end. *[16, 20] sts*

Work in stocking stitch until thumb measures [10, 12]cm ([4, 4¾]in) from tip.

Break yarn and set aside on scrap yarn or a spare circular needle.

Mitten tip

Using MC, and the gauge-sized needles cast on 8 stitches.

Join for working in the round, being careful not to twist the stitches, and place a marker to mark the start of round.

Paw increase

Paw increase setup: K1, m1, k2, m1, K1, pm, k1, m1, k2, m1, k1. *12 sts*

Paw increase round: K1, m1, knit to 1 st before marker, m1, k1, slm, k1, m1, knit to 1 st before marker, m1, k1.

Work **Paw increase round** a total of [7, 9] times. *[40, 48] sts*

Remove the marker added to mark increases (keeping the start of round marker).

Knit [1, 4] rounds.

Cats on paws!

Work the first 24 rounds of the **Cool cats chart**, starting from the bottom right, and working the marked repeat a total of [3, 4] times (see Techniques: Stranded colourwork).

Work round 25 of the chart as follows;

- remove the start of round marker and place a new marker before the final stitch of the last round worked – this is the new start of round marker,
- move the thumb stitches onto the left-hand needle,
- knit the thumb stitches in MC catching CC2 several times,
- then continue knitting row 25 of the chart, placing a second marker after the first stitch of the chart. *[56, 68] sts*

Thumb gusset: part one

For the next three rounds, you will work the main body of the mitten in the chart pattern, knitting the thumb stitches in MC. Make sure to catch CC2 several times along the thumb.

Next round: Ssk, knit in MC until 2 sts before marker, k2tog, slm, work chart row 26 to end. *[54, 66] sts*

Next round: Knit in MC to marker, slm, work chart row 27.

Next round: Knit in MC to marker, slm, work chart row 28.

Break CC2 and work in MC only.

Next round: Ssk, knit until 2 sts before marker, k2tog, knit to end. *[52, 64] sts*

Knit two rounds.

Thumb gusset: part two

Round 1: Ssk, knit until 2 sts before marker, k2tog, knit to end.

Round 2: Knit.

Work **Rounds 1 and 2** a total of [6, 8] times (until all the thumb stitches have been decreased). *[40, 48] sts*

Knit [5, 8] rounds.

COOL CATS CHART

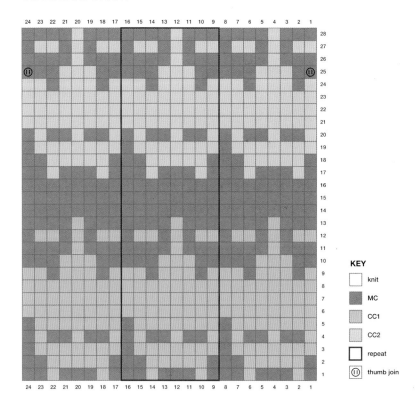

KEY

- knit
- MC
- CC1
- CC2
- repeat
- thumb join

Cuff ribbing

Switch to CC1, and the below-gauge needles, and knit one round.

FOR THE SECOND MITTEN, CONSIDER USING CC2 FOR THE CUFF RIBBING INSTEAD OF CC1.

Ribbing round: (K2, p2) to end.

Work **Ribbing round** a total of 12 times.

Bind off in pattern, using a stretchy bind off method (see Techniques: Stretchy bind off).

Finishing

Weave in all ends, and block.

Don't forget to make a second mitten to match!

Techn

Whenever I meet a new technique I grab some needles and leftover yarn and try it out. If I don't get it perfect first time I can just rip back and give it another go (or ten), without worrying about making a mess of my half-finished knit.

iques

Standard cast on

Make a slipknot on the left needle. Knit into this stitch but do not slip it off the needle. Slip the stitch you've just created to the left hand needle. Repeat!

Loose cast on

Some projects in this book use a loose cast on. This is a standard cast on made using a larger needle size. It's used where the cast on edge will be stitched back to form a hem; the slightly looser edge makes the stitching up a little easier.

Cable cast on

Cast on the first two stitches using the standard cast on method. For the next, and all subsequent stitches, insert the needle between the two last stitches on the left hand needle, and knit one stitch. Slip that stitch back to the left needle and repeat.

Picot cast on

The picot cast on takes a little time, but is absolutely worth the investment.

For a final stitch count with an even number of stitches, cast on four stitches to start, and cast on three if you're aiming for an odd number.

Step 1: Cast on three stitches using the cable cast on method.

Step 2: Bind off two stitches.

Step 3: Slip the remaining stitch back onto the left needle.

Continue working steps 1 to 3 until you have the required number of stitches.

I-cord cast on

The i-cord cast on gives you a neat, knitted edge.

Setup: Cast on four stitches.

Step 1: Knit two stitches, and kfb into the next stitch. There should be one stitch remaining on the left needle.

Step 2: Slip all the stitches back to the left needle.

Continue working steps 1 and 2 until you have three stitches more than required for the cast on. Bind off the first three stitches.

Provisional cast on

There are many provisional cast on methods. This is my favourite, but you can use any method.

You'll need a crochet hook and some scrap yarn. The size of the hook isn't that important as long as you can use it comfortably. A smooth yarn in a contrasting colour makes it easiest to see and undo your provisional cast on.

Setup: Make a slip knot and place it on the crochet hook. Hold the crochet hook at a right angle over the knitting needle.

Step 1: Wrap the yarn around under the needle and over the hook.

Step 2: Pull the yarn through with the crochet hook.

You should now have one stitch on the needle, and one on the hook.

Continue working steps 1 and 2 until you have the required number of stitches on the needle.

Work a couple of extra crochet stitches (not over the needle) and fasten the slipknot loosely – or use a pin to secure it.

You can now start to work those stitches with your working yarn.

When you need to pick up your stitches undo the little crochet chain – start at the end with the extra crochet stitches – and place the live stitches back onto the needle.

Basic bind off (in pattern)

Knit one stitch, knit the next stitch and pass the first knitted stitch over and off the needle.

When a pattern calls for a bind off in pattern this is generally at the end of some ribbing; following the ribbing pattern knit the knit stitches and purl the purls before binding them off.

Loose bind off

Some projects in this book use a loose bind off. This is a basic bind off worked using a larger needle size. It's used where the bound off edge will be stitched back to form a hem; the slightly looser edge makes the stitching up a little easier.

Stretchy bind off (in pattern)

Use this bind off for the brims of hats, the hems or sweaters and the cuffs of sleeves – anywhere you'll need a bit of stretch..

Setup: Work the first stitch (knit or purl as set in the previous row or round).

Step 1: Work the next stitch (knit or purl as set in the previous row or round).

Step 2: If the last stitch was a knit stitch, with yarn at back, insert the left needle into the front of these two stitches, and knit them together through the back loop. If the last stitch was a purl stitch, with yarn at front, insert the left needle into the back of these two stitches and purl them together.

Repeat steps 1 and 2 until all stitches are bound off.

Picot bind off

Step 1: Cast on two stitches using the cable cast on method.

Step 2: Bind off four stitches using the basic bind off method.

Step 3: Slip the last stitch back to the left hand needle.

Repeat steps 1 to 3 until all stitches are bound off.

I-cord bind off

Setup: Cast on three stitches using the cable cast on method.

Step 1: Knit two stitches, and slip-slip-knit the next two together.

Step 2: Slip the three stitches back to the left hand needle.

Repeat steps 1 and 2 until four stitches remain. Bind these off using the basic bind off.

Joining for working in the round

Make sure that the stitches are not twisted; look carefully to check that all the stitches are aligned on the top of the needle, and that the cast on edge doesn't twist over the needle.

Hold your knitting with the needle you'll be working from (the side with the working yarn) in your right hand, and the other in the left.

Then place a stitchmarker onto the right hand needle to indicate the start of round. If you're using DPNs, place a locking stitchmarker onto the cast on edge instead; the change of needles will show you the start of round.

And start knitting! Give a little sharp tug after you make the second stitch, to tighten up the join.

SHORT ROWS

SHORT ROWS DIAGRAMS

Working wraps and turns

When working a knit row or round

Knit to the point where the pattern calls for a wrap and turn.

Keeping the yarn at the back, slip the next stitch purlwise (1). Move the yarn to the front, and slip the wrapped stitch back (2). Turn your knitting ready to work in the opposite direction (3).

When working a purl row or round

Purl to the point where the pattern calls for a wrap and turn.

Keeping the yarn at the front, slip the next stitch purlwise. Move the yarn to the back, and slip the wrapped stitch back. Turn knitting ready to work in the opposite direction.

Working the next row or round

When you come to work a wrapped stitch pick up the wrap and knit or purl it together with the stitch it's wrapped around. Mark your wrap-and-turns with locking markers or bulb pins to ensure that you don't accidentally work past them.

1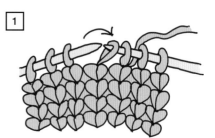

2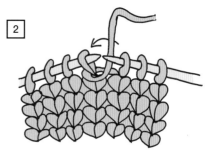

3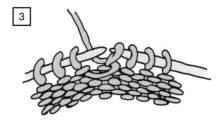

In stranded colorwork you carry the strand of yarn not being knit across the back of the work; the unused strand moves behind the stitches just worked until it's needed.

It's very important to keep your floats relaxed and loose; stretching the last ten stitches of your worked knitting along the needle can help you achieve this. But try to not keep your floats too loose, or they can get caught or snagged when you're wearing your knit.

Swatching and gauge

Your colourwork gauge might be different to your stocking stitch gauge; it's always a good idea to swatch in the colourwork pattern.

Keep your floats as loose as you can – stretching the stitches on the right hand needle can help you manage this, as can working your knitting inside out. For mittens and other small-circumference knits I find it easiest to use a very short circular needle.

Top and bottom yarns

In a stranded knit one colour will be more prominent while the other recedes to the background.

The float of the prominent colour should always be stranded below the background colour. I recommend knitting the emerging cats in the prominent (lower) colour – but whichever way you choose, it's important to keep the upper and lower yarns consistent to avoid tangling.

Managing long floats

For longer floats, trapping them behind a working stitch can improve tension and also keep them from becoming finger-traps. Consider trapping the yarn every four or five stitches in general. In places where the float might easily be snagged (the 'Cool Cats' mittens, for example) every three stiches is probably better, and in places where the float will be safely tucked away (like the 'Cool Cats' cowl) you can keep them a little longer.

Catching the upper yarn on the knit side

Insert the needle into the next stitch.

Wrap both yarns around the needle knitwise.

Unwrap the upper yarn and work the stitch.

Catching the lower yarn on the knit side

Insert the needle into the next stitch.

Wrap the lower yarn around your needle in the opposite direction to the usual method.

Wrap the upper yarn around the needle in the usual method.

Unwrap the lower yarn and complete the stitch.

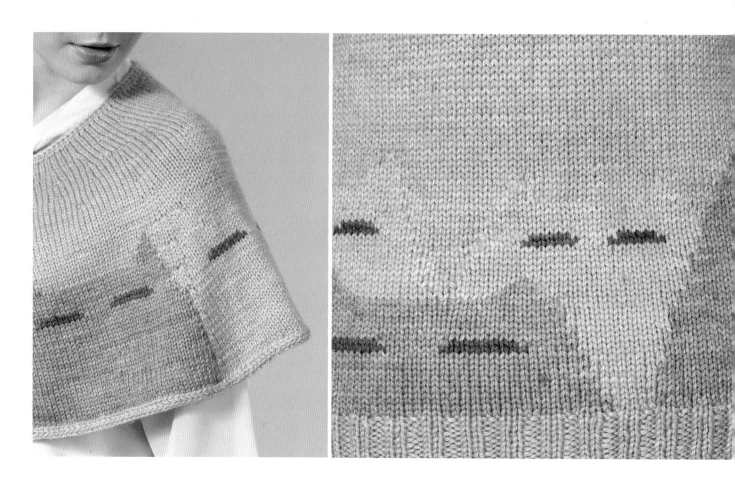

INTARSIA

Intarsia knitting uses blocks of colour to build up a picture. Unlike stranded knitting the unused colour isn't carried along the back; instead, a separate length of yarn is used for each block of colour, and the colours are twisted together at the join.

Estimating yarn

Count over and back across your chart, counting stitches, and noting when each colour ends.

I usually divide these into small, medium and large categories. Any area with less than about 20 stitches is categorised as small, up to about 200 stitches is medium, and more than that is large.

Prepare your yarn

For the 'small' category, cut off a metre or two of yarn. For 'medium', prepare a small ball or bobbin of yarn (10-20 metres) and for 'large' I use a regular ball (or what's left of it after I've removed the small and medium balls.

Knitting the chart

Following the chart, work the first marked stitches in the specified colour, the next in the second color and so on (1).

Leave 10-15cm (4-6in) of tail each time you start a new yarn, and don't cut any ends until you're sure you won't need that strand again. Leave a 15cm (6in) tail when you do snip it off.

Continue working over and back, twisting the yarns around each other when you reach any transition (2). Give both yarns a gentle tug to keep the edge neat.

Cats' eyes

Cut a short strand of yarn (approx 60cm/24in) for each of the cats' eyes for the intarsia patterns – or, to cut down further on the number of strands you're using, omit the eyes when you're knitting the cats and work them in duplicate stitch later on.

INTARSIA DIAGRAMS

1

2

Grafting (Kitchener stitch)

This is a seamless and invisible way to join two sets of live stitches.

Place the stitches to be grafted on two needles. Thread a tapestry needle with the same yarn you used to work your project; you'll need a little over three times the length you're to graft. Hold the needles parallel with the tips aligned.

Setup

Push the tapestry needle through the first stitch on the front needle purlwise, and bring the yarn through, leaving the stitch on the needle.

Push the tapestry needle through the first stitch on the back needle knitwise and bring the yarn through, leaving the stitch on the back needle (1).

The graft

Step 1: Push the tapestry needle through the first stitch on the front needle knitwise, bring the yarn through, and pull the stitch from the needle (2).

Step 2: Push the tapestry needle through the first stitch on the front needle purlwise, bring the yarn through, leaving the stitch on the needle (3).

Step 3: Push the tapestry needle through the first stitch on the back needle purlwise, bring the yarn through, and pull the stitch from the needle (4).

Step 4: Push the tapestry needle through the first stitch on the back needle knitwise and bring the yarn through, leaving the stitch on the back needle (5).

Repeat steps 1 to 4 until one stitch remains on each needle.

Finish off by bringing the needle knitwise through the stitch on the front needle and purlwise through the needle on the back, and pulling them both from the needle (6).

Shoulder seams

Hold the cast on, or bound off edges together, with the right sides facing you, and the stitches lined up. Insert the tapestry needle under a stitch on one side and out again, and then under and out of the corresponding side on the other. Pull together – not too tightly – and repeat.

Side seams

Hold the seam together with the right sides facing you and the stitches aligned. Insert the tapestry needle under and out of the horizontal bar between the first and second stitches. Insert the needle under and out of the corresponding bar on the other side. Pull together – not too tightly – and repeat.

Turned hems and necklines

Fold the hem over, with the folding point at the bottom. Run the needle through the first loop from the cast on edge, and through a stitch just above this. (You'll usually be sewing onto the back of your project, so sewing against a little purl bump). Tug, but not too tightly, and then repeat with the next stitch.

GRAFTING DIAGRAMS

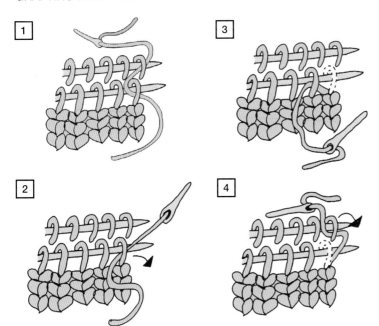
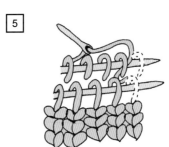
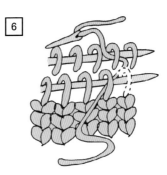

STEEKING

Steeking has a terrifying reputation, but it's really not that difficult – or scary – once you get started. If you're nervous, I can't recommend enough that you steek some swatches to build up your confidence and skill.

You will need: a tapestry needle and some scrap yarn, a crochet hook a couple of sizes smaller than the needles you used. If you've used yarn that's superwash, or not 100% wool, you'll also need some non-superwash wool yarn to work your steek.

Planning your steek

Identify your steek column: a steek usually uses five or seven stitches, and you want to identify the centre stitch of this column (1).

It can be helpful to run a strand of contrasting yarn through the middle of the centre stitches, or to mark them with pins – it's easy to lose your way, especially on dark coloured yarn. A scrap of embroidery thread or crochet cotton is perfect for this, as it won't tangle with your yarn (2).

You'll be working the crochet reinforcement through a half of the centre stitch, and a half of the stitch next to it. If you've been using two colours in your knit, one half of the stitch should be in each colour (3).

Work the crochet reinforcement

Work the crochet chain down from the top right and up from the bottom left (4).

Make a slip knot onto your crochet hook.
Put your hook through the top of the first stitch (5).
Pull through a loop (there'll be two loops on your hook).
Pull your working yarn through these two loops.
Work a single crochet chain down the steek, working in towards the centre of the steek, and secure it at the end.

Snip it

Take a deep breath, and get a small, sharp scissors. Snip slowly and carefully between the crochet chains (6).

That's it!

STEEKING DIAGRAMS

1
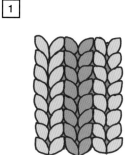

4
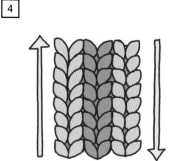

2

5

3
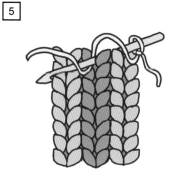

6
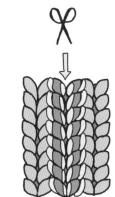

PICKING UP STITCHES

When you get to the button band of a cardigan you know you're nearly finished the knitting! A long and flexible circular needle can make the task much easier, and this method allows you to adjust your stitch count easily.

Identify the columns of stitches you're picking up from between.

Using a long circular needle, slide the needle over the cast on or bound off edge, picking up the first three stitches and skipping over the fourth. Continue picking up three of every four stitches until the whole buttonband or armhole is picked up. Now count your stitches, and adjust the spacing at either end to gain or lose a stitch or two if you need to.

With the right side of the knitting facing you, knit the first row into the back of each picked up stitch. Now you're ready to start working the buttonband or sleeve!

BUTTONHOLES

How big a buttonhole? It depends on the button you use. It can be very useful to work a couple of different-sized buttonholes in your swatch, to either check which one fits the buttons you've chosen or to bring button-shopping.

Calculating buttonhole spacing

You'll need one stitch more than the number of stitches your buttonhole has to work the buttonhole – for example, a four-stitch buttonhole has five working stitches.

Check the number of stitches on your needles, and subtract six (three for the start and three for the end). Then subtract the stitches of one buttonhole. The number you have left is the one you'll be dividing up.

As a starting point for finding a nice, even spacing, plan twice the number of stitches between the buttons as you're using in the buttonhole; for a four-stitch buttonhole, start with a total of fifteen (five for the buttonhole, ten for the spacing). Check if this number divides neatly into your total. You can add or remove a stitch from the top or bottom if you need to. If it doesn't work, try removing or adding a stitch or two to the spacing until you have a nice even spacing.

One-row buttonholes

Knit to the buttonhole. Bring the yarn to the front, and slip the next stitch purlwise. Bring the yarn to the back.

Slip the next stitch, and pass the first slipped stitch over it.

Repeat this until you've slipped as many stitches as your buttonhole needs.

Slip the last slipped stitch back to the left hand needle, and turn work,

Cast on one stitch more than the buttonhole needs, using the cable cast on method. Turn the work.

Slip the first stitch from the left hand needle and pass the last cast on stitch over it.

That's your buttonhole! Work to the next buttonhole position and repeat.

BLOCKING

Blocking your knit helps the stitches to relax, eases out any lumps and bumps in your knitting, and lets you shape it.

You will need; wool wash, blocking mats (or a towel) and blocking pins.

Give your fresh new knit a bath in lukewarm water, with a splash of wool wash. Leave it to soak for about 20 minutes. Rinse it in some more lukewarm water before lifting it out.

Avoid wringing it out – let the water drain – and roll it in a towel. The easiest way to remove excess water is to lay it on the floor and trample on it. Unroll it from the towel again.

Lay your knit onto blocking mats, and pull it into shape. For lacy knits – shawls and cowls – pinning it out under a bit of tension really opens up the lace pattern. For sweaters, or anything where size is important, shape it to the exact dimensions in the pattern.

Leave it to dry – this can take from an hour or so to a day, depending on the temperature and the size of the knit. Once it's dry, unpin it and admire your lovely neat knit!

Cats have a strange affinity for sitting on cold, damp knits, so try lay your blocking out somewhere they can't roll around on your work.

POMPOMS

You will need; scissors, cardboard, yarn and sticky tape.

Cut out two cardboard circles a little larger than you want your pompom. Cut a small wedge from the circles, and a smaller circle in the centre.

TIP: use a glass for the outer circle, and a coin for the inner.

Put a 30cm (12in) length of yarn between the circles, emerging each side of the wedge. Make sure the circles are lined up. Place a piece of tape over the wedges to hold the circles and yarn secure.

Wrap yarn around the circle, covering the cardboard and building up layers. The more wrapping you can do here the floofier your pompom will be.

Cut through the yarn around the edge of the circle. Remove the tape, and tie the yarn secured under it as tightly as you can.

Trim the pompom, making sure to not cut the ends you've tied off. Use these to secure the pompom to your hat.

Tip: Use up leftover yarn scraps and make your cat a pompom to bat about.

About the author

Marna Gilligan is the designer of the Sinister Catdigan; a happy accident where her knitting and cat obsessions melded perfectly (or purrfectly).

She and her two cats live on a boat moored just off the river Thames. You can find snippets of boat- and cat-life on her Instagram feed @ancaitinbeag and see more of her catty creations at https://caitinbeag.com

Suppliers

All of the lovely yarn used in this book was supplied by Eden Cottage Yarns:

www.edencottageyarns.co.uk

Thanks

I still can't believe that this book you're holding exists! And it wouldn't without all of these lovely people:

The team at David and Charles – Sarah, Anna and Jeni – for turning my sketches and ideas into reality.

Charlie, for her glorious obsession with detail editing the patterns.

Victoria and Laura at Eden Cottage Yarns, for helping me find the perfect yarn for every project. My lovely friends, Katie and Sarah, who help me out and keep me sane at yarn shows.

Pete, my best beloved, who listens to my knitty rambles and gives me so much encouragement - even if he still refuses to learn to knit.

And of course, top thanks go to my feline inspirations, Roswell T Catte and Atari Teenage Kitten, for all their help tangling my yarn and sitting on my knitting.

Index

Publishing Director: Ame Verso
Senior Acquisitions Editor: Sarah Callard
Managing Editor: Jeni Hennah
Technical Editor: Charlotte Monckton
Design: Anna Wade
Art Direction: Prudence Rogers
Photography: Jason Jenkins
Design Assistance: Ali Stark
Production: Beverley Richardson
Models: Elisha, Esmeralda & Freya at Gingersnap Models
Fur Models: Petal & Panda

David and Charles publishes high-quality books on a wide range of subjects.
For more information visit www.davidandcharles.com.

Layout of the digital edition of this book may vary depending on reader hardware and
display settings.